Introducing Ethereum and Solidity

Foundations of Cryptocurrency and Blockchain Programming for Beginners

Chris Dannen

Apress®

Introducing Ethereum and Solidity: Foundations of Cryptocurrency and Blockchain Programming for Beginners

Chris Dannen
Brooklyn, New York, USA

ISBN-13 (pbk): 978-1-4842-2534-9   ISBN-13 (electronic): 978-1-4842-2535-6
DOI 10.1007/978-1-4842-2535-6

Library of Congress Control Number: 2017936045

Managing Director: Welmoed Spahr
Editorial Director: Todd Green
Acquisitions Editor: Louise Corrigan
Development Editor: James Markham
Technical Reviewer: Massimo Nardone
Coordinating Editor: Nancy Chen
Copy Editor: Sharon Wilkey
Compositor: SPi Global
Indexer: SPi Global
Artist: SPi Global

Distributed to the book trade worldwide by Springer Science+Business Media New York, 233 Spring Street, 6th Floor, New York, NY 10013. Phone 1-800-SPRINGER, fax (201) 348-4505, e-mail orders-ny@springer-sbm.com, or visit www.springeronline.com. Apress Media, LLC is a California LLC and the sole member (owner) is Springer Science + Business Media Finance Inc (SSBM Finance Inc). SSBM Finance Inc is a **Delaware** corporation.

For information on translations, please e-mail rights@apress.com, or visit http://www.apress.com/rights-permissions.

Apress titles may be purchased in bulk for academic, corporate, or promotional use. eBook versions and licenses are also available for most titles. For more information, reference our Print and eBook Bulk Sales web page at http://www.apress.com/bulk-sales.

Any source code or other supplementary material referenced by the author in this book is available to readers on GitHub via the book's product page, located at www.apress.com/9781484225349. For more detailed information, please visit http://www.apress.com/source-code.

Many thanks to Brandon Buchanan, Christopher McClellan, Dr. Solomon Lederer, and the entire Iterative Instinct team for their support and enthusiasm. Thanks also to Joseph Lubin and the team at ConsenSys for acting as a sounding board during the writing of this book.

Contents at a Glance

Contents

About the Author

Chris Dannen is a partner and founder at Iterative Instinct, a hybrid investment fund focused on cryptocurrency trading and seed-stage venture investments. He first began working with Bitcoin and Ethereum as a miner, and became gradually more enthralled in researching how smart contracts could be used to automate business logic and create new kinds of experiences with software. He was formerly a corporate strategist for Fortune 500 companies. A self-taught programmer in Objective-C and JavaScript, he holds one computer hardware patent. This is his fourth book. Chris is an avid traveler who has trekked across 20 countries, bicycled from Rome to Barcelona in 30 days, and summited Mount Fuji in under six hours. He was formerly a senior editor at *Fast Company* and today consults on technical content for major publishers such as *Quartz* and *Bloomberg*. He graduated from the University of Virginia and now resides in New York, NY.

About the Technical Reviewer

Massimo Nardone has more than 22 years of experience in security, web/mobile development, and cloud and IT architecture. His true IT passions are security and Android. He has been programming and teaching how to program with Android, Perl, PHP, Java, VB, Python, C/C++, and MySQL for more than 20 years. He holds a master of science degree in computing science from the University of Salerno, Italy.

He has worked as a project manager, software engineer, research engineer, chief security architect, information security manager, PCI/SCADA auditor and senior lead IT security/cloud/SCADA architect for many years. Technical skills include security, Android, cloud, Java, MySQL, Drupal, Cobol, Perl, web and mobile development, MongoDB, D3, Joomla, Couchbase, C/C++, WebGL, Python, Pro Rails, Django CMS, Jekyll, Scratch, and more.

He currently works as chief information security officer (CISO) for CargotecOyj. He worked as visiting lecturer and supervisor for exercises at the Networking Laboratory of the Helsinki University of Technology (Aalto University). He holds four international patents (PKI, SIP, SAML and Proxy areas).

Massimo has reviewed more than 40 IT books for various publishing companies. He is the coauthor of *Pro Android Games* (Apress, 2015).

CHAPTER 1

■ ■ ■

Bridging the Blockchain Knowledge Gap

Acclimating to the fast-moving blockchain world can be challenging. This book is your guide. Before we get started, let's define some of the terms you'll encounter ahead

A *blockchain* is a fully-distributed, peer-to-peer software network which makes use of cryptography to securely host applications, store data, and easily transfer digital instruments of value that represent real-world money. *Cryptography* is the art of communication via coded messages. In Bitcoin and Ethereum, cryptography is used to conjur one secure computing environment out of thousands of similar machines, running with no central authority and no single owner. With that kind of potential, it's obvious why the technology has been subject to unprecedented speculation, hype, confusion, and prognostication.

The term "Ethereum" can be used refer to three distinct things: the Ethereum protocol, the Ethereum network created by computers using the protocol, and the Ethereum project funding development of the aforementioned two. On the heels of Bitcoin, Ethereum has become its own macrocosm, attracting enthusiasts and engineers from numerous industries. Many of civilization's most nagging imperfections could become the domain of blockchain's killer apps, and the Ethereum protocol (which was derived from Bitcoin, and extended) is widely considered to be the network where these "distributed" apps will spring up. For developers, designers, and product managers, there's no better time to begin prototyping applications for the Ethereum network.

Blockchain Roll Call!

Two big groups of thinkers are interested in blockchain systems, and Ethereum more specifically: application developers interested in building products and services, and nonprogrammers who are curious about the potential of Ethereum, perhaps owing to work or interest in financial services, consulting, insurance, law, game creation,

© Chris Dannen 2017
C. Dannen, *Introducing Ethereum and Solidity*, DOI 10.1007/978-1-4842-2535-6_1

1

government, logistics, product design, or IT.[1] This book is similarly cross-disciplinary. It provides a contextual guide for programmers and non-programmers alike to develop ideas about what to build, and how to build it. It fills a gap between computer science, economics, financial services, and where necessary, banking history.

For programmers, the challenging thing about Ethereum isn't usually the code; like most open source software projects, this one has on-ramps for people who already program in other environments. Rather, the challenge is wrapping your head around the concept of "cryptoeconomics," or the system of incentives and disincentives which secure the network.

For nonprogrammers, the challenge is divining how the ecosystem will develop, and how you fit in. Claims that blockchains will modernize the banking system, revolutionize insurance, and lay waste to counterfeiting may be overblown—but by how much?[2]

What Ethereum Does

In the abstract, open source blockchain networks such as Ethereum and Bitcoin are kits that allow you to pop up an economic system in software, complete with account management and a native unit of exchange to pass between accounts. Kind of like the game Monopoly. People call these native units of exchange *coins*, *tokens*, or *cryptocurrencies*, but they're no different from tokens in any other system: they're a form of money (or *scrip*) that is usable only within that system.

Blockchains work something like mesh networks or local area networks (LANs); they are merely connected to other "peer" computers running the same software. When you want to make one of these peer-to-peer (P2P) networks accessible through a web browser, you need to use special software libraries such as Web3.js to connect an application's front end (the GUI you see in a browser), via JavaScript APIs, to its back end (the blockchain).

In Ethereum, you can take this concept one step further by easily writing financial contracts with other users inside the system. As you'll see, these financial contracts are called *smart contracts*.

> *The key component is this idea of a Turing-complete blockchain. ... As a data structure, it works kind of the same way that Bitcoin works, except the difference in Ethereum is, it has this built-in programming language.*

—Vitalik Buterin, inventor of Ethereum[3]

In Ethereum, smart contracts are written in the programming language Solidity, which you'll learn about in Chapter 4. Turing completeness was an advantage that many developers quickly latched onto, but more important is Ethereum's ability to save state. In computing, a simple definition of a *stateful* system is one that can detect changes to information and remember them over time.

---

[1]Ethereum Blog, "Visions, Part 1: The Value of Blockchain Technology," https://blog.Ethereum.org/2015/04/13/visions-part-1-the-value-of-blockchain-technology/, 2015.
[2]American Banker, "Blockchain Won't Make Banks Any Nimbler," www.americanbanker.com/bankthink/blockchain-wont-make-banks-any-nimbler-1079190-1.html, 2016.
[3]YouTube, "Technologies That Will Decentralize the World," www.youtube.com/watch?v=er-k3ehpFaM&feature=share, 2016.

Imagine a computer with no hard drive; you couldn't do much with it. It would be like a calculator, the contents of its memory fleeting. The ability to engineer interactions between users in the future, and under certain conditions, is a powerful addition to a blockchain. It allows developers to introduce control flow into cryptocurrency transaction programming. This is the biggest distinction between Ethereum and Bitcoin, but not the only one, as you'll see.

▓ **Note** *Control flow* refers to the order in which computing instructions are executed or evaluated. Examples are conditional statements (if this, then that) and loops (which run repeatedly until certain conditions are met).

In Bitcoin, all transactions happen as soon as possible. Because of Bitcoin's lack of statefulness, it has to execute transactions all in one go. The blockchain as envisioned by Bitcoin's creator(s) was a distributed transaction ledger that kept a running tally of everyone's bitcoin balances in the network. (A stylistic note for close readers: Bitcoin the network is written in the uppercase, and bitcoin the token in lowercase.) In Ethereum, a similar system is made extensible in a standardized way.

Secondarily, this common scripting language makes it more straightforward for blockchains that share the Ethereum protocol to share data with one another, enabling groups that use separate blockchains to share information and value with each other.

WHAT IS A PROTOCOL?

If you're new to software development, a 10-second crash course in information technology (IT) will be useful here. *IT* can be defined as the study of computer systems to store, edit, retrieve, and send information.[4] How that information is represented and updated over time, to reflect changes internal and external, depends on which technological system is in use.

In a telecommunications context, a *protocol* is a system of rules that describes how a computer (and its programmer) can connect to, participate in, and transmit information over a system or network. These instructions define code syntax and semantics that the system expects. Protocols can involve hardware, software, and plain-language instructions. No special hardware is needed for Ethereum, and the software is entirely free.

In Ethereum, the protocol is designed for building decentralized applications, with emphasis on rapid development time, security, and interactivity.

---

[4]Harvard Business Review, "Management in the 1980s," https://hbr.org/1958/11/management-in-the-1980s, 1953.

Three Parts of a Blockchain

A blockchain can be thought of as a database that is distributed, or duplicated, across many computers. The innovation represented by the word *blockchain* is the specific ability of this network database to reconcile the order of transactions, even when a few nodes on the network receive transactions in various order.

This usually happens because of network latency due to physical distance; for example, a transaction created by a user buying a hot dog in Tokyo will be dispatched first to nodes in Japan. By the time a node in New York gets word of this transaction a few milliseconds later, a nearby transaction in Brooklyn sneaks in "ahead" of the one in Tokyo. These inconsistencies due to subjective perspective in distributed systems is what makes them a challenge to scale. The power of blockchain systems is that they represent a combination of technologies we can deploy to crack the problem.

What is widely called a *blockchain* is really the combination of three technologies, a recipe first concocted by Bitcoin's pseudonymous creator. Those three ingredients are as follows:

> *Peer-to-peer networking*: A group of computers such as the BitTorrent network that can communicate among themselves without relying on a single central authority and therefore not presenting a single point of failure.

> *Asymmetric cryptography*: A way for these computers to send a message encrypted for specific recipients such that anyone can verify the sender's authenticity, but only intended recipients can read the message contents. In Bitcoin and Ethereum, asymmetric cryptography is used to create a set of credentials for your account, to ensure that only you can transfer your tokens.

> *Cryptographic hashing*: A way to generate a small, unique "fingerprint" for any data, allowing quick comparison of large datasets and a secure way to verify that data has not been altered; in both Bitcoin and Ethereum, the Merkle tree data structure is used to record the canonical order of transactions, which is then *hashed* into a "fingerprint" that serves as a basis of comparison for computers on the network, and around which they can quickly synchronize.[5]

The combination of these three elements grew out of experiments with digital cash in the 1990s and early 2000s. Adam Back released Hashcash in 2002, which pioneered the use of mining to send transactions. The pseudonymous Satoshi Nakamoto added distributed consensus to this innovation with the creation of Bitcoin in 2009.

Together, these three elements can mimic a simple database that is decentralized and stored in the nodes of the network. In the same way that a group of ants constitute a functioning colony, you can think of Bitcoin as a machine. In computing terms, it's a *virtual machine*, the particulars of which we'll get into later.

---

[5]Wikipedia, "Merkle tree," https://en.wikipedia.org/wiki/Merkle_tree, 2016.

Ethereum adds, in computer science terms, a *trustful global object framework messaging system* to the paradigm established by the Bitcoin virtual machine. Ethereum was first proposed in 2014 with the Ethereum White Paper.[6]

Ethereum Assumes Many Chains

The Bitcoin we know today is not the only large-scale deployment of Bitcoin software. Litecoin, for example, uses the Bitcoin software, modified, as do dozens more. Ethereum was built with the assumption that copycats are a foregone conclusion, and that there may be many blockchains, and thus there should be a set of protocols in place by which they can communicate.

▨ **Note**   Working with the Ethereum protocol benefits from knowledge of both economic and programming concepts. This book contains definitions for both, where necessary.

With a radically different perspective to that of the creators of Bitcoin, the Ethereum creators implicitly took the position that cryptocurrency, if it exists in the future, will not be one decentralized system. Instead, it will be a distributed network of decentralized systems, enabling many different cryptographic tokens of value, with various purposes and interpretations to be easily and quickly defined and then brought to life.

This Is a Scam, Just Like Bitcoin!

If you work in financial services or you studied economics, searching Google for further information has probably brought you to the conclusion that Bitcoin is essentially a global Ponzi scheme. Let's put this to rest.

You are half correct: the value of a bitcoin is determined by the market for bitcoins. Sure, certain bitcoin-holding entities have obtained domestic money transmitter licenses and will redeem your bitcoins for US dollars, Euros, gold, or other fiat currency. But these entities are private businesses that charge fees and could go out of business at any time.

So, Bitcoin and networks like it are vulnerable only to the extent that there is no "redeemer of last resort," no trusted (governmental or corporate) entity you can be sure will redeem your bitcoins or ether for US dollars in the future. Short of paying a private money changer, the only option for converting bitcoins to something of real value is to connect to an online exchange and trade the coins for fiat currency, thus finding another buyer.

Just as the Bitcoin network moves bitcoin tokens, the Ethereum network moves ether tokens. Ether works differently than bitcoin, as you'll see, and can more properly be called a cryptocommodity than a currency. Let's take a look at how the economics of Ethereum relate to the underlying technology.

---

[6]GitHub, "Ethereum White Paper," https://github.com/ethereum/wiki/wiki/White-Paper, 2014.

Ether as a Currency and Commodity

It's commonly said that the bitcoin isn't backed by anything, and that's true. Of course, modern fiat currencies aren't backed by anything either. But they're different: endorsed by a government, a fiat currency is held by default by anyone paying taxes and buying government bonds. Some international commodities sales are denominated in dollars, too (for example, oil) giving people another reason to hold dollars.

For cryptocurrencies, challenges to adoption remain. Today, these digital tokens remain a fast, secure, public payment layer on top of the existing fiat money system; an experimental deployment that might someday grow to replace the centralized payments networking technologies used by companies like Visa and MasterCard today.

However, incredible possibilities are on the horizon as governments and private institutional investors begin to create large markets for financial products and services denominated in cryptocurrencies. Central banks may even adopt the technology. As of this writing, at least one country has issued a *digital dollar* using Bitcoin software: Barbados.[7] Others are actively researching the prospect.

Gresham's Law

Why does it matter if financial products, contracts, insurance policies, (and so on) are being denominated in a cryptocurrency? And what does this have to do with Ethereum?

A currency that can buy a lot of valuable securities and assets is a currency worth saving. The Ethereum network allows anyone to write a trustworthy, self-executing financial contract (smart contract) that will move ether in the future. Conceivably, this could allow financial contracts that project far into the future, giving stakeholders in the contract a reason to hold and use ether as a store of value.

Originally applied to gold and silver currency, *Gresham's Law* states that in an economy, "bad" money drives out "good." In other words, people save and hoard currencies they expect to appreciate in value, while spending currencies they expect to depreciate in value.[8]

Although the law is named for a 16th-century English financier, the concept appears to date all the way back to Medieval writings, and indeed all the way back to ancient texts including Aristophanes' poem "The Frogs," usually dated to around 405 BC:

> *Coins untouched with alloys, gold or silver, Each well minted, tested each and ringing clear. Yet we never use them! Others pass from hand to hand …*

For millennia, people have saved the value of their work-product in a monetary instrument that will stay stable, appreciate in value, or inflate in price—not something prone to crashing in value. Today, cryptocurrencies are volatile in price, and are accepted by only a handful of governments and corporations worldwide as of this writing. Few, if any, decentralized smart contracts are in use in businesses today. But by the same token,

---

[7]Coindesk, "Bitt Launches Barbados Dollar on the Blockchain," www.coindesk.com/bitt-launches-barbados-dollar-on-the-blockchain-calls-for-bitcoin-unity/, 2016.
[8]Wikipedia, "Gresham's Law," https://en.wikipedia.org/wiki/Gresham%27s_law, 2016.

fiat currencies issued by central banks have an awful historical record, demonstrably prone to bubbles, depressions, and manipulation. Can cryptocurrency ever be real money, and will it be better than the money to which we are accustomed?

The Path to Better Money

Today, Bitcoin (denoted by the ticker symbol BTC) is used by people, governments, and corporations to transfer value and buy products or services. Each time they send bitcoins, they pay a small fee to the network, which is denominated in bitcoins. Ether, denoted by the ticker symbol ETH, can be used similarly. To understand the path forward, you need to know a few things.

First, ether has another use: it can pay to run programs on Ethereum's network. These programs can move ether now, or in the future, or when certain conditions are met.

Because of its ability to pay for the execution of transactions in the future, ether can also be considered a commodity, like fuel for the network to run applications and services. So it has an additional dimension of intrinsic value over bitcoins; it is not just a store of value.

Today, the overwhelming usage of fiat currencies might suggest that cryptocurrencies are worse money—that is, more prone to worthlessness in the long run. And yet, bitcoins and ether are famously hoarded by holders, and even held in a trust by at least one company as of this writing: Grayscale, a subsidiary of Digital Currency Group. Meanwhile, central banks in the West experiment with near-zero interest rates and *quantitative easing*, also known as *money printing*, in ever more dangerous and desperate attempts to keep inflation and deflation in check.

With the bitcoin reward halving every four years, global monetary policy woes, general economic uncertainty, and waning confidence in fiat currencies, huge amounts of latent "hoarded" cryptocurrencies are being drawn into the market by higher prices to service genuine demand. This is reflected in the ever-increasing prices of most cryptographic tokens, however volatile their prices intraday. This balancing act between hoarders, speculators, and spenders creates a thriving and healthy marketplace for cryptocurrency, and suggests that *cryptotokens* as an asset class are already serving the purposes of money, and much more.

Cryptoeconomics and Security

One reason to bring up currencies and commodities in the discussion of smart contracts is to train yourself to think in terms of building economic systems in pure software. That's the promise of Ethereum.

The design of software systems with game theoretic rules constitutes the emerging field of *cryptoeconomics*, which we will discuss alongside the technical lessons in this book. What may seem simple at first—an equity coin, for example—creates worlds of complexity when rendered in code. In fact, what makes systems like Ethereum and Bitcoin so secure is that they are not based on any hack-proof technology but rather rely on powerful financial incentives and disincentives to keep malefactors at bay.

These are attractive value propositions that every engineer and software designer should be excited about. But bootstrapping currency (or scrip) coins is an altogether separate, added challenge to getting people excited about end-user applications. This book addresses both halves of the challenge.

7

And although the most obvious applications of this software might be found in financial services, future applications may also use the same levers—trust, transactions, money, and scripting—for entirely other purposes. Just as the command line eventually led to a GUI and now virtual reality (VR) applications, it's up to you to decide what to create with Ethereum. But we'll discuss some examples anyway.

Back to the Good Old Days

It's true that Bitcoin and Ethereum add a bit of complexity—economics—to writing software programs. But they are also simpler in some ways; working with decentralized protocols is similar to working with computers of the 1970s. They were enormous and expensive shared resources, and individuals could rent time on these machines from a university or corporation that owned one. The Ethereum network functions as one large computer which executes programs in lockstep; it is a machine which is "virtualized" by a network of other machines. Being composed of many private computers, the Ethereum Virtual Machine (EVM) itself can be said to be a shared computer which is ownerless.

Changes to the EVM are achieved through *hard forking*: persuading the entire community of node operators to upgrade to a new version of the Ethereum software. Changes to the network can't simply be pushed by the core development team. They involve a political process of persuasion and exposition. This ownerless configuration is meant to maximize uptime and security, while minimizing the incentive for subterfuge.

Cryptochaos

At this point, your head might be spinning. Don't worry—all this information will make more sense when you dive into the specifics in later chapters. Still, never fear: everybody who looks at blockchain development for the first time feels overwhelmed. It's a new technology, things are changing rapidly, and expertise in decentralized systems is rare.

Nobody knows what's coming next, but it's clear the technology is working—to the tune of over $26 billion USD (as of this writing), which is roughly the market capitalization of all cryptocurrencies combined. Retailers big, small, online, and offline are beginning to accept payments in digital coins. (Note that unless otherwise specified, all dollar amounts are denominated in US dollars.)

So, even if you've never programmed before, don't stop here. The Ethereum project is built with new developers in mind, and gives you the tools to create unheard-of solutions to age-old problems. It's up to you to figure out what to build with this powerful new toolset. How to build it, and why you should learn blockchain development are the subjects of the rest of this book.

The Power Is in the Protocol

In today's technology industry, the application layer rules: it's where all the user data lives. Multibillion-dollar companies such as Google, Facebook, and Twitter have built enormous infrastructure to support international user groups. All on top of Transmission Control Protocol/Internet Protocol (TCP/IP), Hypertext Transfer Protocol (HTTP), Simple Mail Transfer Protocol (SMTP), and a handful of other protocols.

In Ethereum, as in Bitcoin, the application layer is thinner, at least so far, because the protocol gives you a lot. In fact, many Bitcoin-based companies to date are fairly minimal layers on top of what is already an incredibly effective payments network.[9]

▨ **Note** *Market capitalization* is a measure of the value of an organization or ecosystem. It is calculated by multiplying the price of one share of the equity for example, one ether) by the number of shares in circulation. Market cap is widely cited as an indication of cryptocurrency adoption; however using *monetary base* might be more appropriate. The monetary base is the total amount of a currency circulated by the public, or held in reserve by institutions that use the currency.

As a result, the Bitcoin startup explosion that so many venture capitalists anticipated just five or six years ago never came. Instead, the Bitcoin industry went quickly into consolidation.[10] But the market capitalization of Bitcoin as a network has ballooned to almost $19 billion in less than a decade. The market cap of Ethereum is about $1 billion. This is an unprecedented, fast new way to bootstrap a new network protocol.[11]

Traditional web applications are costly in large part because they must be engineered to store and exchange user data, and thus must have systems in place to isolate bad actors in order to elicit trust. Many private data centers operate behind bomb-resistant defensive landscaping and layers of razor wire. When the security offered by these layers of private infrastructure can be exceeded by a secure decentralized network, the operators of online businesses experience drastically lower overhead costs, which they can pass on to customers to disrupt legacy players. Blockchain-based apps and services are disruptive not only because of their secure nature, but because of how economical they can be to operate at scale.

You Can Build Trustless Systems

Once you learn the Solidity language, you will quickly get to wondering what kind of programs you can write—and that is where the real learning curve sets in. The goal of the projects in this book is to show exactly how, and where, blockchains can improve or automate the end-user experience of all sorts of businesses, and enable the creation of new kinds of products and services. You will see how the banking products and services we know today, which evolved over a thousand years of trial-and-error, can change, benefit, or be brought to scale by trustless distributed or semidistributed systems. *Trustless* is used in this context to mean

---

[9]USV Blog, "Fat Protocols," www.usv.com/blog/fat-protocols, 2016.
[10]Daily Fintech, "Bitcoin Market Going into Consolidation Before Product Market Fit," https://dailyfintech.com/2016/02/03/bitcoin-market-going-into-consolidation-before-product-market-fit/, 2016.
[11]Coinbase Blog, "App Coins and the Dawn of the Decentralized Business Model," https://medium.com/the-coinbase-blog/app-coins-and-the-dawn-of-the-decentralized-business-model-8b8c951e734f#.cweqnimd2, 2016.

"not requiring faith that counterparties will operate honestly and without failure, thus impervious to fraud and other counterparty risks."

There is already some good information on the Web about Ethereum and Solidity for software developers looking to get started. However, if you've read these docs, you were probably left with more questions than answers. Next, we'll clarify some jargon.

What Smart Contracts (Really) Do

Even in just these first few pages, you may have encountered some wildly new concepts. But there's one term which will continue to pop up in Ethereum, and that is the notion of a smart contract: some business logic that runs on the network, semi-autonomously moving value and enforcing payment agreements between parties.

Smart contracts are often equated to software applications, but this a reductive analogy; they're more like the concept of *classes* in conventional object-oriented programming. When developers speak of "writing smart contracts," they are typically referring to the practice of writing code in the Solidity language to be executed on the Ethereum network. When the code is executed, units of value may be transferred as easily as data. As stated in this chapter already, the promise of digital money is immense. But how does it work, exactly? How can data act like money in a decentralized system?

The answer to that question depends on how technical you are. So let's take a fairly in-depth example.

Objects and Methods for Value

In computing, an *object* is usually a little chunk of data—information—encapsulated in a particular structure or format. Often this data has associated instructions called *methods* indicating how the object can be used or accessed. Now let's imagine the information held in this object is valuable to someone, and this person would be willing to pay to trigger a method which displays it.

In the example below, let's imagine a user wants to pay a small fee to use a cake recipe he or she discovered online. This recipe is the data object in our example. At the most literal level, the characteristics of the cake object, called *attributes*, are stored along with the methods at a certain address in the computer's memory.

The object below represents the attributes of a cake, and contains a method whereby the computer can display instructions for how to combine these ingredients to make the cake. Storing the information in this way makes it easy for the program and the programmer to swap in and out the attributes without needing to change the code for the display instructions. In other words, objects are modular chunks of information which can be combined and recombined to suit. This will be important to remember in later chapters when we discuss the anatomy of the *blocks* that comprise the blockchain. In JavaScript, you can write a cake object as follows:

```
var cake = {
firstIngredient: "milk",
secondIngredient: "eggs",
```

```
thirdIngredient: "cakemix",
bakeTime: 22
bakeTemp: 420

mixingInstructions: function() {
return "Add " this.firstIngredient + " to " + this.secondIngredient +
" and stir with " + this.thirdIngredient + " and bake at " + bakeTemp +
" for " + bakeTime + " minutes." ;
}
};
```

This is an example of how computers "move" data around to display useful results to their human users. In Ethereum, you can write functions that send money around, just as this little object's method called mixingInstructions, when executed, can display the mixing instructions for a cake.

Just Add Commerce

As you'll see in Chapter 4, Solidity code can be used on the back-end of an application to add micro-payments, user accounts, and functionality to even simple computer programs, without the need for third-party libraries or advanced programming know-how.

Imagine for a moment that the mixingInstructions function cost a few cents in ether to execute. After the price of the cake recipe is deducted from the user's Ethereum wallet balance—which takes a few seconds, on average—your smart contract would call the mixingInstructions method and show the user how to make the cake. All this can be done without authentication, payment APIs, accounts, credit cards, extensive web forms, and all the typical work that comes with building an e-commerce application. In fact, all your JavaScript application needs to interact with the global public Ethereum chain is that software library mentioned earlier, Web3.js.

Content Creation

So far in this chapter, we've focused on the pecuniary uses of ether, but the cake recipe example showcases another big area of potential for Ethereum: intellectual property, licensing, and content royalties. Today, selling content on the Web or through apps means dealing with powerful distributors including Apple, Google, and Amazon, who make punitive rules about selling digital content and levy large fees.

Ethereum makes it possible to facilitate microtransactions whereby a user pays only, say, $0.25 for a recipe—an amount that would be impractical to pay using fee-laden credit-card networks. There are challenges to content creators doing business this way today, including the price volatility of the ether token, but as you'll see in subsequent chapters, these issues will find resolution as the network matures.

11

Where's the Data?

Hang on: if the network protocol provides so much functionality out of the box, and this is a distributed system, where is the user data held? Exactly how the Ethereum network works is the subject of the next chapter, but in the spirit of addressing nagging questions first, here's a quick run-down of how transactions are recorded in Ethereum: *it's all stored on every node of the network.*

All transactions in Ethereum are stored on the blockchain, a canonical history of *state changes* stored on every single Ethereum node.

When you pay for computing time on the Ethereum network, this includes the cost of running the transaction and for storage of the data included in your smart contract. (If your contract gets smaller after executing, you'll get a partial refund in the form of a reduced transaction fee.)

As soon as you execute your smart contract and the fees are paid from your ether balance, that data will then be included in the next block. Because the Ethereum network requires all nodes to keep a full state database of all contracts, any node can query the database locally. If this sounds unscalable, you are paying good attention. Ethereum versions 1.5 and 2.0 define a roadmap that addresses this scalability issue.

We'll get deeper into how the Ethereum blockchain works in the next chapter.

What Is Mining?

Because a distributed system has no single owner, machines are free to join the Ethereum network at will and begin validating transactions. This process is known as *mining*. But to what end?

Mining nodes confer to arrive at a consensus about the order of transactions across the system, which is necessary to tabulate everyone's account balances on the fly, even as many transactions pass through the network. This process consumes electricity, which costs money, and so miners are paid a reward for each *block* they mine: about 5 ether.

Ether and Electricity Prices

Miners are paid this ether for mining, and also for running scripts on the network (in the form of *gas*, which will be explained later). The cost associated with electricity expenditure of servers running on the Ethereum network is one of the factors that gives ether, as a cryptocommodity, its intrinsic value—that is, someone paid real money to their electricity company to run their mining machine. Specialized mining rigs, which use arrays of graphics cards to increase their odds of completing a block and getting paid, can run up electricity bills anywhere from $100 to $300 a month per machine, depending on rates in your area.

Mining is fundamental to both Bitcoin and Ethereum, and in principle works similarly in both networks, with a few caveats. Ethereum has revised the paradigm here too, especially around the issuance of ether. How exactly this works is the subject of Chapter 5.

Going Inside the EVM

The goal of this book is to teach programmers and product owners how the Ethereum Virtual Machine (EVM)—the name for the system just described—can be programmed, and to what ends. It is written in a way that should make sense to both financial and technical thinkers, so that developers and domain experts can more easily arrive at a common understanding of what they should build together, and which tools are right for their project. But first we'll need to spend some time on the basics of using and holding ether.

■ **Note** If you're not sure what a *virtual machine* is, don't worry; it will become apparent later. For now, you can think of it as a computer comprising many other computers.

The Mist Browser

At this stage, deploying applications is still difficult, but there are ways to prototype smart contracts simply, with just the Solidity scripts. To do this, you'll use the native Ethereum browser, nicknamed *Mist*. This browser also holds your ether. Chapter 2 covers more about wallets, browsers, command-line tools, and blockchain explorers, but first a note on terminology.

Browser vs. Wallet or Keychain

Mist is sometimes referred to as a *wallet*, a term borrowed from Bitcoin parlance. Why are Bitcoin applications called wallets? Not because they hold your money, although wallet apps do let you send and receive payments. These applications, when installed on your phone, are issued cryptographic keys that allow you to read and write data to a decentralized database. So although *keychain* might be a better metaphor, *wallet* is the term we got.

If you want to jump ahead and check out Mist, you'll find the download for Mac, Windows, and Linux on the Ethereum GitHub project: https://github.com/Ethereum/mist/releases.

With Mist and the Ethereum command-line tools, sample contracts can be tested with fake ether to ensure that you don't lose any real money while debugging. And although doing this feels a bit primitive if you've used modern development environments, it's a great starting point for less-technical learners, because it forces them to learn about networking and low-level computer systems just to make a simple demo app.

Solidity Is Kind of Like JavaScript, But …

Written in a vacuum, much of Solidity is intuitive for anyone familiar with JavaScript, Java, or C languages. Although Ethereum applications aren't hosted on any single server, the guts of an Ethereum app are a series of (relatively) simple smart contract files that look like JavaScript. You create them locally before deploying them to propagate around the whole network to be hosted in a decentralized manner. In this sense, Ethereum development combines both networking, app hosting, and databasing into one.

Like many new technologies, deployment of these systems is challenging. We'll talk about some ways to make it easier. But after creating your first minimally functional application, you'll quickly hit the fun part: imagining what new applications and systems are possible with your new skills.

What Ethereum Is Good For

Ethereum is suited to building economic systems in pure software. In other words, it's software for business logic, wherein people (users) can move money (data representing value) around with the speed and scale that we normally get with data.[12] Not the three- to seven-day floating period you get with the commercial banking system. Or the fees associated with vendors such as Visa, MasterCard, and PayPal. With a simple Ethereum application, for example, it is fairly trivial to pay hundreds of thousands of people, in hundreds of countries, small amounts every few minutes, whereas in the legacy banking system you would need an entire payroll department working overtime to constantly rebalance your account ledgers and deal with the cross-border issues.

A Critical Take

If you've looked at the marketing for Ethereum, you probably have a slightly more dramatic vision of what this software can create. Here is a selection of starry-eyed declarations about Ethereum, and the blockchain in general, with obvious and common rebuttals.

"Without any possibility of downtime, censorship, or third-party interference"

If you aren't familiar with the world of open source development, then the way the codebase is governed will appear obscure at first. Even though the Ethereum protocol was written by a small group of core developers, many classes of stakeholders must cooperate to change the way the network functions, now that it is up and running. As the network grows, these so-called *hard forks* will become less feasible and less necessary, and therefore less frequent. Remember, the Ethereum network is not yet complete. It is operational today, but will not be complete until sometime in 2019. Funds for continued development are endowed to the Swiss nonprofit Ethereum Foundation.

---

[12]Ethereum Blog, "The Business Imperative Behind the Ethereum Vision," `https://blog.Ethereum.org/2015/05/24/the-business-imperative-behind-the-Ethereum-vision/`, 2015.

"A secure, free, and open platform for the Internet of Things"

Machines may be the executors of many smart contracts, so the thinking goes. Let's say you wander into a neighborhood you've never been to, and you lose your cell signal. Your phone might automatically "rent" some time off a nearby femtocell in another network, and pay the router a tiny fee, all without needing to ask your permission. The price and speed might be variables in a smart contract authored by the router, almost like a service-level agreement (SLA) that can move money when you agree to it.

"Enabling transparent governance for communities and businesses"

Okay, this one is tricky: transparent companies are a likely outcome. But decentralized autonomous companies (alternately referred to as DAOs or DACs) are probably a long way off. The term used in this book is the one the industry seems to be settling on: *decentralized organization*, or *DO*. Progress in this area is tricky. Governance by way of cryptographic instrument is subject to all the same manipulations that have plagued democracies for ages. Is one vote one wallet address? Well, who gets a wallet address? If a coin is a vote, do rich people rule? That conversation is mostly outside the bounds of this book, but anyone selling you on the concepts of fully autonomous organizations, corporate or governmental, probably also has a bridge you might be interested in.

"Handles user authentication and secure payments for you, as well as messaging and even decentralized storage"

This one will be fully true when Ethereum is further along its roadmap. User authentication and secure payments are indeed in the box when you connect to the Ethereum blockchain, but peer-to-peer communication and decentralized storage (itself a nascent segment of blockchain software businesses) is presently available with only third-party integrations. However, the Ethereum roadmap does include these elements as planned under the names Swarm and Whisper. Both are currently available in limited experimental versions.

"No need to sign up or pay for application host; the world's first zero-infrastructure platform"

Technically true, but time is money, and as we discuss hosting and deployment, it will be clear that *free* and *straightforward* might be mutually exclusive terms in this new software world.

State of Smart Contract Development Today

Few sample projects for Solidity development are available today. If you're thinking about deploying a full end-user application, you won't have much competition. Yet.

However, most of the power of the blockchain is in creating applications enabling users to make transactions: buying, selling, licensing, trading, streaming, and so forth. This means people need to be holding some ether, or a native coin belonging to your project. The circulation and availability of such a native coin is called its *liquidity*. High liquidity can also lead to more-stable prices in a currency and has network effects.

Often, entrepreneurial-minded developers will attempt to bootstrap their coins into circulation to achieve the benefits of liquidity. Indeed, the EVM and ether work exactly this way. The Ethereum Foundation was crowdfunded to the tune of $18 million upon launch in 2014. Contributions paid in bitcoins were returned in ether, and a community was born.

Copycat Coins

Alt-coins are Bitcoin copycats that use the Bitcoin codebase. There can be legitimate reasons to start an alt-coin; they're not always attempts to brute-force a user base into existence.

Ethereum retains many of the underlying concepts of Bitcoin, but can be considered an altogether new network, as its key components are different.

Funding Your Project

Crowdfunding is one way for entrepreneurs to combat the pain and expense of live beta testing and fundraising, by selling early access to a product or service to prospective users. In cryptocurrencies, this is called a *token launch*. Some companies have adopted the term *initial coin offering* (*ICO*), because it sounds like the Wall Street term *initial public offering* (*IPO*). However this term is misleading, as tokens do not always represent equity. This holds for both ether and bitcoins, which do not represent equity in anything.

If you're thinking of raising money to fund your Ethereum project, you don't need to fly by night. Asset managers and executives are quickly waking up to the power of this technology, and whether you are looking for employment, investment, or business development, it's out there (or will be soon). Look for local Bitcoin or Ethereum events on Meetup (www.meetup.com) to find other cryptoenthusiasts and form a team.

Deciding Where You Fit In

In addition to covering the technical aspects of Ethereum, this book presents a wider array of contextual information that can help you decide how Solidity programming and distributed applications should fit into your career. This book also aims to identify new vectors for innovative thinking about software.

One example is longevity. In legacy web services, uptime depends on whether developers have paid their hosting bills and maintained their servers. As a result, few people build software applications meant to execute commands in, say, 30 years.

The Ethereum network is also a fully redundant distributed database, with copies on every node. That means you can trust your application to fire off a call when a certain condition is met, even if that condition happens decades into the future—and even if the nodes have all changed.

The removal of the old constraints of software and banking, and the introduction of new ones, are constant themes in every chapter ahead.

A Note to New Programmers

Knowing how the existing monetary, banking, and insurance systems work will be of enormous advantage when imagining applications for Ethereum. If you can combine that with some technical knowledge, all the better.

■ **Note**   You don't have to dog-ear the URLs or references in this book. You'll find up-to-date links for all the citations in this book, indexed by chapter, at http://eth.guide.

So even if you're not a programmer, and you don't intend to become one, follow along in the sections that discuss code anyway. It will help you grasp the limits of what's possible. And if you do decide to learn Solidity programming from scratch—having never programmed—this book's lessons are accessible to you, too.

In some ways, learning Ethereum development may be easier and more intuitive than learning web development from scratch.

Ethereum Is Free and Open Source

Ethereum can be forked and replicated into other systems that remain compatible. In the future, it may even be possible for coins to be transferred from chain to chain. Although this is far from a straightforward process, academic papers about how it may be done are already emerging.

It's worth noting, for the nonprogrammers reading, that *free* and *open source* are not synonymous. Open source is a methodology for creating software; freedom is a social construct. According to the GNU Foundation, "When we call software *free*, we mean that it respects the users' essential freedoms: the freedom to run it, to study and change it, and to redistribute copies with or without changes."[13]

The EVM Is Here to Stay

As you'll see, Ethereum has an ambitious roadmap and even more ambitious goals. Whether it develops as the core development team plans, its lasting contribution to blockchain development may be the EVM. The Solidity language may become one of many that compile down to EVM bytecodes.

Solidity itself will no doubt grow and change, and it's far from perfect or complete today. But it allows us to build and test use cases for cryptocurrency now, in ways which arguably would happen slower in the Bitcoin community.

---

[13]GNU Foundation, "Why Open Source Misses the Point of Free Software," www.gnu.org/philosophy/open-source-misses-the-point.html, 2016.

In short, Ethereum seeks to create a system in which economic models can be tried and proved. For the time being, Solidity looks poised to become the de facto language of such models, as long as they are run on a global virtual machine such as the EVM.

What You Can Build Today

Enough talk about potential; what is possible today? Quite a lot, but let's break things down into two categories: private and public. So far, Ethereum has been described both as a single public blockchain, and a protocol for the creation of many blockchains. Understanding the potential in different domains (and how it might manifest) is mostly a question of understanding how the public chain differs from private Ethereum chains, deployed by corporations or other silo'd communities.

Private and Public Chains

Because anyone can fork the Ethereum project, it's possible to "make your own Ethereum" rather than building on the public chain. This is called a *private* blockchain, and like Bitcoin's alt-coins, it represents a duplication of effort by the existing Ethereum development community.

As you'll discover by the end of this book, private chains are generally a terrible way to do things for a startup product or service, but that hasn't stopped some companies from trying to launch one. Instead of reinventing the wheel, a better idea for entrepreneurs is to build on top of the public Ethereum chain.

As you'll see, the public chain has a lot of computing power dedicated to its security, making it fairly turn-key for small companies to launch large-scale secure web services. However, the public Ethereum blockchain today is entirely public, and some corporations may choose to keep their sensitive transactions on a private chain, which has some bridge to the public chain. In an enterprise software context, where corporate stakeholders are given certain rights and privileges to read and write to the company chain, the deployment is known as a *permissioned blockchain*. For permissioned blockchains, wallet addresses are typically issued by a trusted third-party who verifies your permission to enter the system, just the way an office building's security pass allows you to transact inside the building. By the same metaphor, the public chain would be considered a city park or other common space.

The positive correlation between a blockchain's scale and its trustworthiness will become apparent in later chapters. However, we will walk through the setup of private chains in Chapter 9 to gain a better understanding of the similarities between blockchains and databases.

In both public or private Ethereum chains, you can do the following:

- Send and receive ether
- Write smart contracts
- Create provably fair applications
- Launch your own token based on ether

Each is described in the following subsections.

Send and Receive Ether

You can send and receive ether, though on a private chain you have private ether that's a value-less scrip. Anyone can get a public Ethereum wallet address by downloading the Mist wallet, which we'll cover in the next chapter. Alternatively, mobile wallet applications are available in both the iOS App Store and Google Play. In order to trade dollars for ether, you need to join a cryptocurrency exchange, or buy from a commercial money transmitter such as Coinbase. Most people simply buy bitcoins (which are more widely available in ATM form, and also through the LocalBitcoins.com cash dealer network) and convert them to ether via an exchange or via a cryptomoney-changing service such as ShapeShift.io.

Write Smart Contracts

You can control payments and transfers between accounts (and even between other contracts) even if they have lots of contingencies, or extend far in the future and across national borders. The true potential here rests on how unstoppable the public chain really is, and that depends on who is participating and how many bad actors come into the system. Alternately, private chains may allow groups with resources the same functionality, just privately.

Create Provably Fair Applications

Creating provably fair applications is especially important for gaming and gambling. Expect video games and virtual reality games to introduce points that represent real money and can be spent in the real world.

Launch Your Own Token

In practical terms, rolling your own token is something like spinning up a system of user accounts.

With an Ethereum token contract, you can create a *subcurrency* for use in a private transaction ledger, accessible to only you and your private group, but that uses the public chain in all other ways—forgoing the need to fork or maintain your own network of mining machines. This is convenient, and a superior approach for most developers and organizations. The dynamics of tokens and chains will become clearer in Chapters 5 and 9.

The Promise of Decentralized Databases

Like all databases, a blockchain has a schema: rules define, constrain, and enforce relationships between entities. Motivations to break or alter these relationships can be found across industries, leading to bribery and corruption, and making blockchain's trustless qualities even more attractive to business than prior generations of software and networking.[14]

---

[14]Nesta.org.uk. "Why you should care about blockchains: the non-financial uses of blockchain technology," http://www.nesta.org.uk/blog/why-you-should-care-about-blockchains-non-financial-uses-blockchain-technology, 2016.

In all databases, shared read/write access creates enormous complexity. Machines all over the world may experience varying latency, depending on where the database is physically located, leading to some write operations arriving out of order. This gets even more difficult if several parties are supposed to equally share a database; for example, several companies forming an industry trade group. This has made it extremely expensive for large organizations to enable shared read/write status with other organizations, and today, the leaking of customer information is all too common.

Today, corporate IT departments have found ways of mostly making sure these systems work as planned. But as they scale, the opportunity for malfeasance becomes too large for some bad actors to ignore.

What's Next: New Ways of Working

In September 2016, thousands of employees of Wells Fargo bank were fired for manipulating account databases to juke sales numbers and trigger bonuses intended to reward salespeople opening new accounts.[15] The costs of those errors in judgement will be enormous, as will the cost of building software that can somehow prevent administrators from making erroneous changes. Ethereum represents a new opportunity for businesses and consumers to interact in a more trustworthy milieu than the application data layer that has been built on the HTTP web today.

Summary

In this chapter, you learned that Ethereum offers another approach to building software, one in which security and trust are baked in at the protocol level. This may have a substantial global impact. As the world digitizes, large-scale systems become increasingly mission-critical for all kinds of organizations—not just in banking and insurance, but also in city services, retail, logistics, content distribution, journalism, apparel manufacturing, and any other industry that has provenance or payments in play.[16]

Next, you'll get hands-on with Ethereum by creating keys to access the Ethereum blockchain through programs known as *clients*. The next chapter covers using Ethereum client apps for Windows, macOS, Linux, iOS, and Android.

---

[15]CNN Money, "5300 Wells Fargo Employees Fired Over 2 Million Phony Accounts," http://money.cnn.com/2016/09/08/investing/wells-fargo-created-phony-accounts-bank-fees/, 2016

[16]Daily Fintech, "How Blockchain Technology Could Integrate Financial & Physical Supply Chains and Revolutionize Small Business Finance," https://dailyfintech.com/2016/06/14/how-blockchain-technology-could-integrate-financial-physical-supply-chains-and-revolutionize-small-business-finance/, 2016.

CHAPTER 2

The Mist Browser

In the realm of cryptocurrency software, there are generally two essential types of client applications: wallets and full nodes

> **Note** Wallet usually denotes a lightweight node that connects to a blockchain to perform basic functions, such as sending and receiving cryptocurrency. Full nodes are command-line interfaces that can perform the full gamut of operations allowed by the network.

As we covered in the last chapter, *Ethereum* can refer to both the Ethereum protocol and the Ethereum network created by computers using the protocol. Operating a node on the network allows you to upload smart contracts. For sending and receiving cryptocurrency (in our case, ether) all you need is a wallet application for your computer or smartphone.

Ethereum has several client applications that are discussed in this book. The most useful (for most readers) is the Mist browser, a user-friendly wallet that can perform some of the duties of a full node—namely, executing smart contracts.

Eventually, entire web-app-like programs will be accessible through Mist, with their back ends built on Ethereum; that's why it's called a *browser*. Don't be fooled by Mist's simplicity. Today, it's useful for sending and receiving the ether cryptocurrency. But tomorrow, it may also be a distribution point for consumer and enterprise software applications, almost like an App Store.

> **Note** The term *currency*, as in *cryptocurrency*, refers to a fungible unit of value for the system, much like a token, or *scrip*. What exactly these little tokens represent will become clear later in this chapter. The term fungible, applied to a currency, means "mutually interchangeable." In fiat currency terms, one dollar can be said to be fungible for another dollar.

© Chris Dannen 2017
C. Dannen, *Introducing Ethereum and Solidity*, DOI 10.1007/978-1-4842-2535-6_2

In this chapter, you'll learn how to access the network by using Mist and other applications, in order to understand the basics of sending and receiving ether tokens between accounts. Subsequent chapters break down how the system works and how to program smart contracts for it.

Wallets as a Computing Metaphor

Wallets are software applications for desktop or mobile devices that hold your *keys* to the EVM. These keys correspond to an *account*, which is referred to by a long account address. In Ethereum, accounts do not store your name or any other personal information. They are pseudonymous. Anyone can generate an Ethereum account by connecting to the network with any Ethereum client (such as Mist). You can generate as many as you'd like.

If you've already downloaded an Ethereum wallet or full node on your computer or phone, you were probably prompted to create an account. The wallet application probably also asked you to create a password to protect your keys with encryption. As you can gather, these keys are an important part of sending and receiving ether.

Let's begin by looking at your account address, also called a *public key*. Your public key has a matching *private key* that allows access to your account. This private key should be kept secret and not published anywhere.

Accounts in both Bitcoin and Ethereum are represented by long hexidecimal addresses. An Ethereum address looks like this:

0xB38AA74527aD855054DC17f4324FE9b4004C720C

In the Bitcoin protocol, the raw hexidecimal address is encoded in base 58 with a built-in version number and checksum, but underneath looks just like an Ethereum address. Here's an example of a Bitcoin address:

1GDCKfdTo4yNDd9tEM4JsL8DnTVDw552Sy

To receive ether or bitcoins, you must give the sender your address, which is why it's called a public key. Of course, these strings are not memorable. If you're new to programming, you might be wondering what's going on here; why the unwieldy alphanumeric mess? Experienced programmers may already know that these public and private keys are part of asymmetric key cryptography.

Your Address Is What?

Why do account addresses—which are meant to be public, and which some people even list on their web sites—consist of such long, cryptic strings? Why can't we just have usernames?

The answer is that someday soon you probably will be able to generate plain-English usernames, but they'll function more like top-level domain names today. You'll rent a name from a decentralized network registrar, and it will redirect to your real account address, much the way that top-level domains redirect to IP addresses today.

A lot of plans for the Ethereum network are in the pipeline that will eventually replicate the niceties of today's HTTP Web as we know it. To learn more about the Ethereum roadmap, skip to Chapter 11.

■ **Note**   An *account* is a data object: an entry in the blockchain ledger, indexed by its address, containing data about the state of that account, such as its balance. An *address* is a public key belonging to a particular user; it's how users access their accounts. In practice, the address is technically the hash of a public key, not the public key itself, but for simplicity, it's better to ignore this distinction.

In the EVM, asymmetric cryptography is used by the network to generate and recognize valid Ethereum addresses, and also to "digitally sign" transactions. In secure communications, asymmetric cryptography is used to *encipher* private communications, so that even if they are intercepted by enemies, they remain unreadable. In blockchain the principle works the same; it's a method for ensuring that messages (in the form of EVM transaction requests) are coming from the actual address holder, and not an interloper trying to hijack their funds.

Where Is My Ether?

It's important to note that ether is not contained in any particular machine or application. Your ether balance can be queried, and ether sent or received, by any computer running an Ethereum node or wallet. Even if the computer where your Mist wallet lives gets destroyed, never fear: all you need is your private key, and voila, you can access your ether from another node.

However, if you hand over your private keys to someone else, that person can access the EVM and pull your money out without you ever knowing. As far as the network is concerned, *anyone with your private key is you.*

Because the EVM is a global machine, it has no way of knowing which node you'll create a transaction from. Unlike today's web apps, Ethereum does not look for a "trusted" computer; it doesn't know your phone from any other phone. If this seems unusual, think of it like a bank ATM system, which provides account access for anyone holding your debit card number and your four-digit pin.

As mentioned in Chapter 1, losing your phone or computer to theft or destruction *does not mean you lose your money*, provided the following are true:

You have backed up your private key.

You didn't give your private key to anyone else.

Backing up a private key is as simple as copying and pasting it into a text file, and saving it on a USB stick. Or writing it down on paper. You'll find more private-key backup methods later in this chapter.

The Bank Teller Metaphor

In a way, using a wallet or full node is like getting behind the bank teller's desk and being in control of your own money. Not in the sense that you can get paper cash, but in the sense that a bank teller *controls a node within the bank's computer system that can execute transactions in a global database of transactions.* A teller controls the bank's database, which connects to other bank databases.

In conventional banking, by extension, a paper check is a written instruction for the bank teller to make a transaction using the bank's computer system. On the check is your account number and a routing number. (We'll talk more about the conventional banking system in the next chapter.)

For now, it's only important to point out that buildings full of people (plus vast computing resources) are required to take your paper check, turn it into an electronic transaction, send the transaction to another party, and then update the balances of both parties. In cryptocurrency, this legacy banking system—a hodgepodge of human and computer processes—is completely obviated by the use of an algorithmic consensus engine running on a peer-to-peer computer network. Settlement and clearing of transactions happens on the network itself within seconds (or, with bitcoin, minutes) of the transaction being digitally signed and broadcast by a node. Thus it can be said in in cryptocurrency transaction that "the settlement is the trade."

In Cryptocurrency, You Hold Your Own Assets

Cryptocurrencies are different from the fiat currencies used by conventional banks, which are centralized. Your tokens are virtual, and your balance (along with that of everyone else who holds ether) is tabulated by the blockchain network. There is no tangible ether or bitcoin currency, although some third parties have created "collectible" coins preloaded with cryptocurrency.

Be extremely wary of any online service or organization that offers to hold, store, or act as custodian of ether, bitcoins, or any other cryptocurrency. The advantage of distributed public systems is to eliminate counterparties from transactions, and allow entities to transact on a peer-to-peer basis. The point is, you can hold these assets securely, without a custodian.

That said, we live in a fiat currency world. Even if cryptocurrencies are indeed the future (and as you'll see in this book, there is stupendous evidence they are) perhaps several years or more will serve as a transitional period, wherein people have both a cryptocurrency wallet and a traditional bank account.

To summarize: *Do not use any wallet or online service that holds your private keys for you.* Only use applications that store your private keys on your device. Later in this chapter, you'll find recommendations for desktop and mobile wallets. Let's get back to explaining the purpose of Mist as your first gateway to the EVM.

Visualizing Ethereum Transactions

The best way for new Ethereum programmers to visualize the concept of a blockchain is to imagine a paper transaction ledger that can be synchronized with other paper transaction ledgers around the world.

When a wallet application attempts to make a change to the database, the change is detected by the nearest Ethereum node, which then propagates the change around the network. Eventually, all the transactions are recorded on every ledger.

In the abstract, this works something like the polygraph machine patented by John Isaac Hawkins in 1803. This was the first "copy machine," although its name today is used to refer to so-called lie-detecting devices. This duplicating machine, famously praised by Thomas Jefferson as the finest invention of its day, is shown in Figure 2-1. Just like the polygraph, the blockchain is an apparatus for allowing many "machines" to change the state of a ledger in the same way, nearly simultaneously.

Figure 2-1. *The polygraph machine is similar to the blockchain in principle: many machines working in concert to write similar data to similar local databases. In Bitcoin and Ethereum, the technological innovation lies in the fact that these state changes can come in out of order, owing to network latency, and the network can reconcile them into a single ledger.*

As mentioned previously, your address is sometimes called your *public key*, but a better metaphor would be a lockbox with a unique serial number. The private key is the only thing in this whole system that is named sensibly: it unlocks your account and allows you to move ether out.

What is *ether*, exactly? It's merely a balance in your account. When you send and receive either, nothing is actually sent or received.

In the EVM, when one account increases, the system makes sure it's because another account has sent a payment, and thus decreased the same amount. It's a closed system. It's practically impossible to give yourself free ether, or at least it wouldn't be worth the costs you'd incur trying falsify the ledger. Ethereum uses financial incentives and disincentives for security, as you'll see in Chapter 7.

Breaking with Banking History

One of the most interesting facets of the Ethereum protocol is its issuance scheme, which will be discussed later. For now, it's only important to point out that (as with Bitcoin) no individual has the power to create more ether. This characteristic stands in stark contrast to the last 400 years of financial markets and central bankers, which reads like a history of large-scale scam artists.

Since the stock-jobbing days of the late 17th century in London's Exchange Alley, entrepreneurs and scammers (then called *stock projectors*) have been selling equity in ventures both legitimate and not. Often they would secretly issue new shares to themselves and their confederates when the price would go up—known to Americans in the 19th century as *watering* the stock.

Over time, speculating on stocks became a pastime that people of all ages and backgrounds enjoyed on both sides of the Atlantic, and the modern stock markets were born, with their processes and *counterparties* to act as middlemen who ensure trustworthy transactions. But even with the banking regulations passed after the Great Depression, dishonest entrepreneurs still found ways to carve out secret stock pools, or unload the shares they had without the public knowing—only to let the business collapse after getting their money out.

Few times in modern history have speculative bubbles wiped out as much wealth and human progress as the crash of 1929 in the United States. However, similar depressive episodes in the United States and Europe (including the Panic of 1873–1879) were caused by someone, either central banks or investors themselves, messing with the base quantity of money, equities, or bonds in a large marketplace.

How Encryption Leads to Trust

Chapter 1 breezed past any real discussion of cryptography, and focused instead on the impact of crypto-networks. But, there's something strange about a secure network comprised of a bunch of strangers' PCs working in concert. How come a single bad apple can't hack the network and steal everyone's ether? To answer that question, first recall that a blockchain uses the following methodologies:

  Asymmetric cryptography

  Cryptographic hashing

  Peer-to-peer distributed computing

Let's spend some time briefly talking about the first item on this list: asymmetric cryptography, which is sometimes broadly called public-key cryptography. A quick detour here will help us better grasp how a public network can be secure. We'll address the other two elements in Chapter 6.

Asymmetric cryptography is a method of sending secure messages back and forth over a network, where the sender and the recipient do not trust the channel of communication. In the case of the EVM, those messages are transactions, being signed and sent to the network in order to change the state of some of its accounts. It's called "asymmetric" because each party has a pair of two different, but mathematically related, keys.

Public-key cryptography was developed for wartime communications, and when used properly, can be extremely secure. Unlike *symmetric*-key cryptographic, public key cryptographic communications don't require a secure channel between parties. This is essential in Bitcoin and Ethereum, because any computer running the protocol can join the network, without any vetting. However, the computational complexity involved in encrypting data makes it useful only for small data objects, like the alphanumeric string that becomes your private key. This is why encryption must be used sparingly.

At a high level, it can be said that Ethereum uses encryption to validate and verify that any and all changes made to account balances in the EVM are legitimate, and that no account has been increased (or decreased) erroneously.

If you're new to computer science, the very mechanism of encryption might be hazy. For the time being, here are some definitions that will help moving forward:

> *Symmetric Encryption*: A process by which a snippet of plain text, usually held in a document, is smashed together with a shorter data string called a *key* to produce a ciphertext output. This output can be reversed, or *decrypted*, by the party that receives it, so long as they also have that same key. Trying to decode the message without the key would be, computationally speaking, immensely time-consuming and expensive—so much so that some kinds of encryption are considered practically unbreakable, even with huge computing resources.

> *Asymmetric encryption*: This way of encrypting information requires the program to issue two keys simultaneously, one that is public and one that you keep private. The public key is public in the sense that you can list it on your web site or social profile, such as an e-mail address. (When communicating, parties can use one anothers' public keys to encrypt information, as described below.)

> *Secure Messaging*: In our first example, Alice uses Bob's public key to encrypt a message. When he receives the ciphertext, he can decrypt it using his matching private key, ensuring that only Bob can read the message. This is called secure messaging. But it leaves a dangerous possibility open: anyone could send Bob a message claiming to be Alice. How does he know that Alice is the real sender of the message?

> *Secure and Signed Messaging*: If Alice wanted to assure Bob that she is the true sender, she would do things differently. First, she would take her plaintext message and encrypt it using her private key. Then, she would encrypt it again using Bob's public key. When Bob receives the message, he decrypts it first using his private key, but he's still left with ciphertext. He must decrypt it again using Alice's public key. This second layer of encryption assures him that Alice is indeed the sender, because presumably, nobody has Alice's private key but Alice. This is known as "secure and signed" messaging.

If Alice were to only encrypt her plaintext using her own private key, then anyone with her public key could decrypt it. This is known as an "open message format" because, while it proves the identity of the sender, it can be decrypted by anyone.

Digital signature: For maximum security, Alice would take another step: she would hash the plaintext of her message, and attach it along with the message. She would then encrypt this bundle with her own private key, and again with Bob's public key. When Bob receives and decrypts the ciphertext he can run Alice's plaintext message through the same hashing algorithm Alice used. If for some reason the fingerprint of the message turns out differently, then it means the actual message text was damaged or altered en route.

As you'll appreciate more in Chapter 6, which covers mining, the method by which individual transactions are broadcast to the EVM is similar to the description of the digital signature above, where the contents of the transaction are hashed and enciphered before being broadcast to peers. Now that you can appreciate the security of the Ethereum network, let's get to the brass tacks of Mist installation.

System Requirements

Most users will opt for the Mist browser, but this section lists other tools that developers may find just as interesting. Mist makes it easy to send and receive ether. It also contains an interface for executing smart contracts quickly and easily. We'll talk more about how to run contracts in Mist in Chapter 4.

Mist runs well on a modern computer with at least 2 GB of RAM and 30 GB of hard disk space free. For lower-performing machines, try the MetaMask Chrome extension. It's described later in this section.

You'll find the latest version of Mist on the Ethereum project GitHub site (`https://github.com/ethereum/`).

More about Eth.guide and This Book

Because Ethereum is a new and fast-moving project, some of the project and documentation links may change after the publication of this book. For this reason, commonly needed links and references for this book are also listed at `http://eth.guide` and updated regularly with new material. Similarly, all footnoted links are indexed on this page by chapter, and updated if and when they change.

To make the site more useful as a reference, subdomains have been created for popular topics. You'll see these shortcuts mentioned throughout the text.

The Eth.guide site is linked to the GitHub project for the book itself, so you will also find the sample code projects from this book at the same URL. The full URL for the GitHub project for this book is `https://github.com/chrisdannen/Introducing-Ethereum-and-Solidity`.

If you're a nontechnical reader just looking to get started with the basics, go ahead and skip to the section entitled "Finally, into the Mist!" Developers, read on to see what other tools to peruse at this stage of your Ethereum journey.

Tools for Developers

Developers will want to check out these three tools in addition to Mist:

- MetaMask Chrome extension (useful for everyone)
- Geth (useful for intermediate developers)
- Parity (useful for advanced developers)

The Chrome extension MetaMask is the simplest way to get up and running with Ethereum. It lets you execute smart contracts and transactions right in your browser without needing a full Ethereum node. MetaMask has the power to create accounts, and to send and receive ether. You can download MetaMask from the Google Chrome Add-Ons menu, or by navigating to the project URL at `https://metamask.io/`.

For all its convenience, MetaMask does not download the entire blockchain to your computer; nor can it mine transactions and earn ether. However, these are minor drawbacks for users just looking to get up and running with Ethereum quickly.

MetaMask was built by Aaron Davis (a.k.a. Kumavis) of ConsenSys, an Ethereum development and consulting company whose free tools you'll encounter frequently in this nascent Ethereum blockchain space. ConsenSys is a 60-person Ethereum venture studio and consulting company in Brooklyn, NY, run by Ethereum project cofounder Joseph Lubin.

MetaMask was funded in part by development grants (DEVgrants) from the Ethereum Foundation. These grants are open to anyone working on an Ethereum project, and do not require the project creator to give up any equity. To learn more about DEVgrants, visit the program's Gitter channel at `https://gitter.im/devgrants/public` or follow its Twitter handle @devgrants.

CLI Nodes

If you already know you want to begin development with Solidity, download a full command-line node. The most popular command-line interface (CLI) nodes for the Ethereum network are written in Go and C++, and they're called Geth and Eth (alternately, `go-ethereum` and `cpp-ethereum`).

■ **Note**   Because there are many Ethereum clients for various operating systems, this book uses the most straightforward development environment: Ubuntu 14.04 running Geth. Mac or Windows users may want to try installing a virtual machine such as VirtualBox that can run an Ubuntu instance.

Advanced developers may also want to pair Geth with Parity, a super-fast Ethereum client written in the Rust programming language. In the Chapter 6 we'll talk about basic Geth commands.

Recommended: Using Parity with Geth

Ethcore.io is a private Ethereum development company composed of a few former contributors to the Ethereum project, including Gavin Wood, another Ethereum project cofounder, who created the Solidity language and authored the Ethereum Yellow Paper.[1]

He and his team have created a powerful node written in the Rust programming language. Parity works on macOS, Windows, Ubuntu, and in a Docker instance. You can find out more by checking out the GitHub project at https://github.com/ethcore/parity.

░ **Note** If you plan on using a Mist wallet through your Parity node, you'll need to manually start Parity before you open Mist. Otherwise, Mist will connect via its own node. Under the hood, the Mist browser runs a Geth node.

Detailed step-by-step instructions for setting up the Mist wallet with Parity running on the back end are available on YouTube from the Ethcore team (www.youtube.com/watch?v=sta-p5d1blQ).

Finally, into the Mist!

Now that you have a better sense of what an Ethereum client does, let's put one on your computer. The Mist browser is compatible with Linux, macOS, and Windows computers with both 32- and 64-bit architectures. If you don't know whether your computer is 32- or 64-bit, check your system's hardware profile. Most newer systems are 64-bit.

Downloading and Installing Mist

First, download Mist from https://github.com/ethereum/mist/releases, as shown in Figure 2-2.

---

[1]Gavin Wood, GitHub, "Ethereum Yellow Paper," https://github.com/ethereum/yellowpaper, 2014.

Downloads

⏻ Ethereum-Wallet-linux32-0-8-4.deb	42.3 MB
⏻ Ethereum-Wallet-linux32-0-8-4.zip	61.8 MB
⏻ Ethereum-Wallet-linux64-0-8-4.deb	41.7 MB
⏻ Ethereum-Wallet-linux64-0-8-4.zip	61 MB
⏻ Ethereum-Wallet-macosx-0-8-4.dmg	59.9 MB
⏻ Ethereum-Wallet-win32-0-8-4.exe	60.7 MB
⏻ Ethereum-Wallet-win64-0-8-4.exe	85.7 MB
⏻ Mist-linux32-0-8-4.deb	41.7 MB
⏻ Mist-linux32-0-8-4.zip	59.6 MB
⏻ Mist-linux64-0-8-4.deb	41.2 MB
⏻ Mist-linux64-0-8-4.zip	58.8 MB
⏻ Mist-macosx-0-8-4.dmg	58.6 MB
⏻ Mist-win32-0-8-4.exe	58.8 MB
⏻ Mist-win64-0-8-4.exe	83.8 MB
⎙ Source code (zip)	
⎙ Source code (tar.gz)	

Figure 2-2. *From the Ethereum project on GitHub, click to download the executable for your OS, or download the source code to compile it yourself*

You'll find this download link among the other client downloads at:

`http://clients.eth.guide`

On Windows, double-click the executable that downloads. On macOS, open the disk image that downloads and drag the Ethereum wallet to your Applications folder. On Ubuntu, download the Debian package or unzip the zip file and open it to install.

■ **Note** It's not possible or advantageous to run more than one node at once. If, for example, you try to open Geth while Mist is already running, you'll get an error telling you a node is already operational on your machine.

Configuring Mist

After you download and open the installer, you'll see a welcome screen like the one in Figure 2-3. (There are some of those big promises from Chapter 1!)

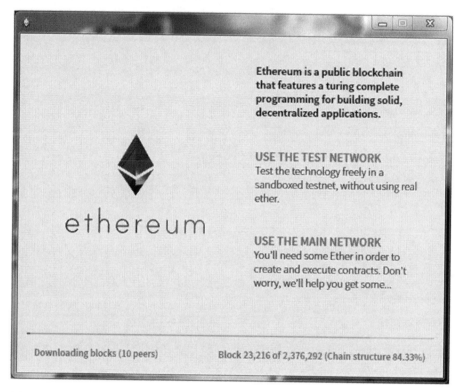

Figure 2-3. The main network is also known as the main chain. The test network is a sandbox environment for playing with fake ether and debugging contracts.

Here you'll be asked which chain, or network, you want to connect to. At this stage, it doesn't matter which one you choose; you'll be able to switch networks later. But for our purposes, let's make you a real wallet address: click Use the main network.

Notice the bottom of the window, which indicates *downloading blocks*. This application runs a full node on the Ethereum network; that means it keeps its own copy of the blockchain, which it must first download before any real action can take place. This will take a long time, because the blockchain contains a record of every transaction ever on the Ethereum chain.

Next you'll see the screen shown in Figure 2-4, which you can skip—unless you participated in the Ethereum crowdsale back in 2014. In that case, follow those instructions to redeem your ether.

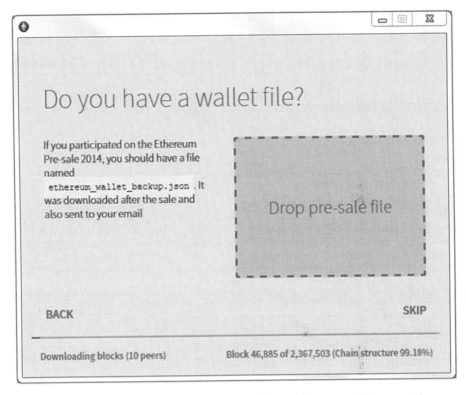

Figure 2-4. *The Ethereum crowdsale, which entitled participants to a file representing ether, took place in 2014. Click the Skip option if you didn't participate.*

After you pick your password, as seen in Figure 2-5 (and write it down or memorize it), you'll see a prompt that requires some explaining.

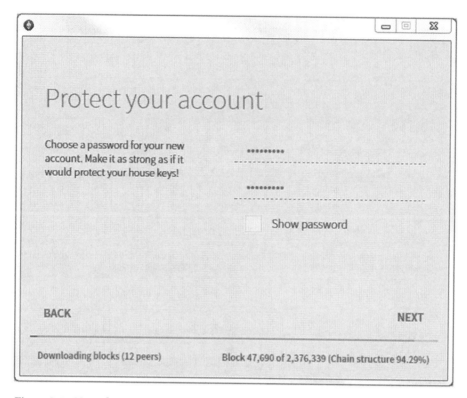

Figure 2-5. Next, choose a password

■ **Note**   There is no Forgot Password functionality in the Ethereum network. That's because your password is only for this local instance of the Mist wallet; it's not saved on the Ethereum blockchain. In fact, your private key is all you need to re-create this account on any other computer running Mist. The password you create merely protects you from an interloper sitting down at your computer and spending your money through the Mist interface. It does not stop anyone from stealing your private keys from your computer's file system, if it's left unprotected. Take precautions, such as turning of the Automatic Login at Startup feature on your Mac, Linux, or Windows PC.

On the next screen, shown in Figure 2-6, you'll get your first glimpse at your *etherbase* address, which is like the Ur-address for this machine as long as this node and its data are intact. If you delete the Mist application and its data from your system library, this public-private key pair—your etherbase—will be deleted. That's why it's necessary to back up your accounts, which we'll go over at the end of this chapter.

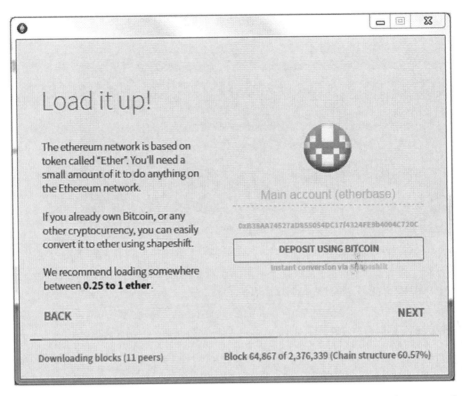

Figure 2-6. Here you can see the new address. You can also deposit bitcoins to be converted into ether by the Shapeshift.io API.

Finally, you'll see the screen in Figure 2-7 as the blockchain syncs to your computer. If you click Launch Application, the Mist interface will load. Don't be distressed if your new account doesn't show up yet. It will appear when the node is fully synchronized.

Figure 2-7. This will take a while. Your new account will show up when it's done.

Finding Your New Address

You can create more addresses, but they will all exist under the aegis of this etherbase address, which makes backup easier.

If you click through the following screens, you'll notice these are just time-killers to let you learn more about Ethereum while the blockchain downloads. If you're curious, click any of the examples in these screens to see the contract code.

Sending and Receiving Ether

Sending ether requires first holding some ether. On the main network, tokens either cost money or can be mined. However, this is an unwieldy way to get started for most Ethereum beginners.

We've gone ahead and created an account on the main network, just in case you're interested in holding real ether for speculative value, or if you already have friends and collegues who use it for payments. For most readers, using test ether (which you can generate for free on the testnet, dubbed Ropsten) is better than paying money for real ether for use on the main network. Instructions for connecting to Ropsten are presented in Chapter 5.

For now, it's worth describing how ether is sent and received, without going through the motions, because it will help clarify the way the underlying system works. Ether is sent via the Send dialog box, shown in Figure 2-8.

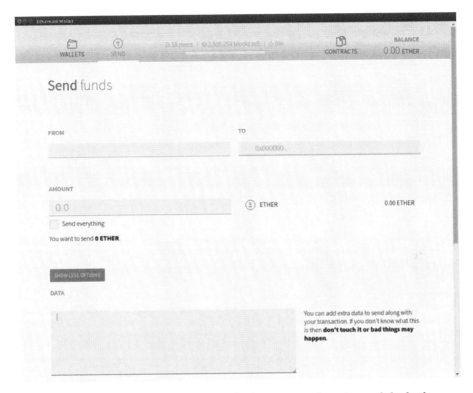

Figure 2-8. *The Send dialog box in Mist makes it easy to send, receive, and check ether balances without using a command-line interface.*

To send ether, you follow these steps:

1. In real life, ask the recipient for their Ethereum address.

2. Open Mist. Click Send in the top bar of the Mist wallet. The Send dialog box opens.

3. Choose which wallet you would like to send from,

4. Paste in the recipient's address.

5. Enter the amount.

6. Click Send.

You'll notice two more options that you can toggle: a data field for entering extra text (for example, an order number or thank-you note) and a slider bar for choosing a transaction fee. The purpose of transaction fees will become clearer in Chapter 6. For now, leave the slider in the default position, and your transactions will process just fine.

▓ **Note**   For practical purposes, when sending ether, your Mist wallet must be fully synchronized. That means that you may need to wait some time for Mist to download the blockchain before you can be sure your transactions will process without an error. As you'll see later, this isn't technically required; recently offline nodes are indeed capable of initiating transactions, but only if the user creates the transaction in the command line, with up-to-date information about the account in use.[2]

To receive ether, your node does not have to be synchronized. If you'd like to check your balance, you can safely click Launch Application and skip the synchronization process when Mist launches.

Understanding Ethereum Account Types

Users interact with the Ethereum blockchain through accounts. In Ethereum lingo, accounts created and used by humans are called *externally owned accounts*. This is in contrast to *contract accounts*, as in an address that is occupied by a smart contract.

▓ **Note**   External accounts aren't always controlled by humans. Sometimes they're controlled by trusted endpoints somewhere else. The point is, they're external to the EVM.

If this distinction is confusing, remember that contracts can take actions in lieu of people in the Ethereum network. You can send value (ether) to people or you can send it to a smart contract, which will take some automated action. For example, a remittance contract might take the sender's deposit, split it in three, and send the amounts onward to three different human relatives. In this way, contracts can act in lieu of humans to automate tasks within a decentralized organization or to mediate transactions between individuals that would otherwise need a counterparty.

▓ **Note**   Both contract accounts and external accounts are state objects. *Contract accounts* have both account balance state and contract storage; *external accounts* have only balance state. However, it's important to note that there is currently a development proposal under review by the Ethereum development community for more abstraction in the EVM. It's intent is to abstract out the duality we have today by turning all accounts into smart contract themselves. This way, users are free to define their own security model.

---

[2]StackExchange, "When Transferring Ether, Who Needs to be in Sync with the Blockchain," https://ethereum.stackexchange.com/questions/2273/when-transferring-ether-who-needs-to-be-in-sync-with-the-blockchain, 2016.

To review some of the basics:

- A key pair is issued when you register a new account.

- You can register for as many accounts as you like.

- Creating an account (a key pair) can be done by any Ethereum node (even when it is offline).

- There is no master list of key pairs or accounts anywhere on Earth.

- Account numbers are not associated with you, your identity, or your computer.

- You can access the Ethereum network with your private key from any computer running an Ethereum node.

Backing Up and Restoring Your Keys

While in the Mist browser, and after Mist has completed synchronizing to the blockchain, go to the File menu of your operating system and choose the Accounts menu, then Backup Accounts. This opens a folder. Inside this folder are text files that have long names starting with the date of creation, such as UTC--2016-09-01 (...) Each of these plain-text files represents an account.

Back up this keystore folder by zipping it and putting it somewhere safe, such as a USB key or encrypted hard drive.

If you open one of these text files, you will find your private and public key pair, formatted in a certain notation.

To restore an account on a different node than it was created upon, simply locate the keystore folder by the same method described previously. Instead of duplicating the files already there, restoring an Ethereum account in Mist simply involves copying a text file containing a private key inside the keystore folder, and restarting Mist. For a full tutorial, visit http://backup.eth.guide and http://restore.eth.guide.

If you'd like to find the keystore folder on your hard drive via the terminal, it's usually located in the following directories:

- Mac: ~/Library/Ethereum/keystore

- Linux: ~/.ethereum/keystore

- Windows: %APPDATA%/Ethereum/keystore

The preceding process will back up only your normal accounts. Wallet contracts are held in the data folder, so (once you've done the exercises in later chapters) back that up as well:

- Mac: `~/Library/Application Support/Mist/`

- Linux: `~/.config/Mist` or, in earlier versions, `~/.config/Chromium/Mist` (folder is hidden)

- Windows: `C:\Users\< Your Username >\AppData\Roaming` or `~\AppData\Roaming\Ethereum\keystore`

Each time you create a new account in Mist, be sure to grab the key file and back it up!

Using Paper Wallets

You may have spotted in the preceding section that an Ethereum node doesn't need to be online to create an account. This has to do with the way the Ethereum network generates addresses; it can create a new and valid key pair with near-zero chance that key pair already exists.

This characteristic of the system allows for something most web applications can't offer: a "paper" account. Sites such as MyEtherWallet (`www.myetherwallet.com`) allow users to create a key pair right in the browser, stored locally on the machine. This site also makes it easy to print your key pair on paper, for safekeeping.

This is called a *paper wallet* because it contains a Quick Response (QR) code, allowing people to make deposits to your Ethereum account simply by snapping the QR code on the paper sheet. In theory, you could go around collecting Ethereum payments this way, but you'd need to put that private key into an instance of Mist (or another client) to access that ether and send it anywhere else.

Using Mobile Wallets

There are a growing number of mobile wallet applications for iOS and Android that store private keys on the mobile device itself. The most popular and trustworthy to date is Jaxx, shown in Figure 2-9, which is made by a Canadian software company called Decentral. Their software runs on Mac, Linux, Windows, and even a few other platforms including Firefox and Chrome. Decentral is operated by Ethereum project cofounder Anthony Di Iorio.

Figure 2-9. Jaxx is probably your best bet for wallet applications that run on iOS and Android. It holds bitcoins, ether, and a selection of other cryptocurrencies.

The basic interface layout you see in Figure 2-9 has become a fairly standard UI in wallet applications. Users are presented with their wallet addresses, and can view those same addresses as QR codes. The QR codes make it easier to send ether or bitcoins in person, much the same way that Snapchat uses QR codes to allow users to follow each other by simply snapping the other user's code. Here you'll find a list of trustworthy wallet applications: http://wallets.eth.guide.

Before going any further, it's worth mentioning that an understanding of QR codes is all that's needed to participate in the cryptoeconomy. To send someone ether or bitcoins with a mobile wallet, you click Send, scan the other party's QR code (or paste in their public key) and enter an amount. They'll receive their ether within seconds.

Working with Messages and Transactions

In both Ethereum, *transactions* are used to refer to state changes in the distributed database (that is, in the blockchain). Transactions change account balances within the EVM. *Messages* are data objects passed back and forth across the network between smart contracts, and do not necessarily result in any changes being made on the chain. For example, if one contract checks the balance of another.

Transactions Change State

A *transaction* in Ethereum refers to a piece of data bearing a cryptographic signature, which goes in the blockchain, and is thus recorded on every node in the network. Every transaction triggers a message to accomplish this state change, but messages are also sent by EVM code. These messages are private to the parties and are not represented in the blockchain.

Editing a Global Database

One reason that blockchain networks like Ethereum are touted as immutable is that once a transaction is written to the global shared database, it cannot be reversed by any other transaction. In modern payments terminology, this is known as a system without chargebacks.

A *chargeback* in North American payment channels is defined as the forcible return of funds to an account holder, initiated by the issuing bank of the instrument. Because Ethereum has no central issuing authority, there is no one to appeal to if you mis-key a transaction. Presently, the only way to roll back a transaction is a state fork, which requires all nodes on the network to agree to manually revert a transaction. This is an extremely difficult and unlikely scenario reserved for network-wide attacks of one form or another.

The reason for this transaction model is security. Compare sending cryptocurrency from one account to the other, to the process of writing a conventional paper check. In the latter example, your bank receives news of the outgoing transaction from your account. The bank first checks your balance to see whether you have the funds to pay the amount you endorsed on the check; if you don't, the depositor's bank does not increase the deposit account. Instead, you are issued a fee for writing a bad check.

Transactions in the Ethereum network work similarly. The system ensures that the outgoing amount from one account is always added to the destination account. If for some reason the destination account can't be accessed—say because the cryptographic signature is not valid—then the source account doesn't have its balance decremented, and thus funds are not lost. In Ethereum, externally-generated transactions are always signed cryptographically with the keys of the sender and the recipient, making it straightforward to ensure that bad actors can't create transactions, and money can't be lost just because of a mis-keyed address.

So, What Is a Blockchain?

So far we've carefully avoided breaking down the concept of blocks, and focused on how transactions are initiated. Next we'll discuss how those transactions are cleared and settled by the network. A *block* is a unit of time that encompasses a certain number of transactions, just as a heartbeat is a period of time in which a certain quantity of blood is moved through an animal's body. Inside that period, transaction data is recorded; when the unit of time elapses, the next block begins. The *blockchain* represents the history of state changes within the network database of the EVM. To quote the Ethereum docs:

> *The blocks on the blockchain represent units of time; the blockchain itself is a temporal dimension and represents the entire history of states at the discrete time points designated by the blocks on the chain.*[3]

Smart contracts may be uploaded to the network in a given block, but may not actually send any messages or transactions until a much later block.

Paying for Transactions

When a human sends a transaction, the EVM requires a tiny fee to process the transaction. This works similarly for the uploading of smart contracts: users must pay for the computational effort the EVM will expend running each contract. By forcing users to pay for transactions on the EVM, the likelihood of wasteful never-ending programs being executed is theoretically reduced. These costs are priced in a unit called *gas*.

You can think of gas as a metric indicating the number of steps the EVM will have to take to complete the instructions in the transaction. If this is a simple instance of one person sending money to another, the transaction fee will be cheap, because this requires a small number of computational steps. In the case of a complex smart contract, however, the fee will be higher, because the EVM has to use its global resources to execute the Solidity code in the contract and figure out what transactions to then execute as a result.

Transaction senders are required to include a *gas limit* that says how much they're willing to pay to have their transaction executed. Full nodes on the network which are *mining*, or securing the network for pay, provide the hardware for these many transactions to be collated, validated, cleared, settled, and stored within the blockchain, thus they receive the transaction fees a user pays when he or she sends ether to a friend, or executes a smart contract. Miners who execute the transaction collect the fee, so an implicit market process is at play. Whether or not a transaction executes is determined by the amount of gas the sender is willing to pay. If the total number of steps exceeds the gas budgeted for a transaction, all steps are rolled back, and no part of the transaction is executed. If a user sends a transaction with too low a transaction fee, it will be processed only after some time, or not at all.

---

[3]Ethdocs.org, "Account Types, Gas, and Transactions," http://ethdocs.org/en/latest/contracts-and-transactions/account-types-gas-and-transactions.html, 2016.

For context, it's true that every operation costs some amount of gas; most operations cost 1 unit of gas. A complex transaction can cost hundreds of units of gas. However, in dollar terms, this adds up to very little.

Understanding Denominations

Like fiat currencies, ether balances and values have standardized denominations for small units. All ether balances are typically denominated in ether, and remainders are denominated in *wei*. For example, 10.234 ether = 10,234,000,000,000,000,000 wei.

If you think of ether as dollars, wei are like dimes, quarters, pennies, and nickels. Table 2-1 details the wei denominations.

Table 2-1. *Denominations of ether. In the Unit column at left, the equivalent bitcoin denominations are provided in parentheses*

Unit	Wei Value	Number of Wei
Wei	1 wei	1
Kwei (babbage)	1^3 wei	1,000
Mwei (lovelace)	1^6 wei	1,000,000
Gwei (shannon)	1^9 wei	1,000,000,000
Microether (szabo)	1^{12} wei	1,000,000,000,000
Milliether (finney)	1^{15} wei	1,000,000,000,000,000
Ether	1^{18} wei	1,000,000,000,000,000,000

You can find an ether denomination converter tool at http://ether.fund/tool/ converter.

Getting Ether

The easiest way to obtain ether is to convert bitcoins inside the Mist wallet, as described earlier in this chapter. You can earn ether by mining, but as mentioned previously, this requires initial setup; you can't mine from within Mist, unless it's on the testnet. (This has to do with the way smart contracts are tested and executed on the network, as you'll see in Chapter 5.)

If you'd like to buy ether with fiat currency, such as US dollars, you need to do so on an exchange or with a licensed money transmitter. To see a table of online platforms that sell ether, see http://vendors.eth.guide.

Testnet ether is free, as stated earlier in this chapter. Instructions for getting test ether from a "faucet" are in Chapter 5, with more details about creating transactions.

Anonymity in Cryptocurrency

Bitcoins and ether are not anonymous payment instruments. Anyone who knows your public key can look on the blockchain and see the dates and amounts of transactions coming in and out of your account. From this data, they might be able to put together a pattern of transactions from which they could deduce your activities. Federal authorities are already using machine-learning transactions to decode spending patterns on dark-market sites such as AlphaBay.[4]

Anonymity, secrecy, and privacy in cryptocurrency are generally conflated by newbies, sometimes with disastrous ends. Bitcoin and Ethereum addresses are pseudonymous by nature; they're not linked to your real name or information. But every transaction you send is public, in the sense that anyone can see the transaction on the blockchain. This is why public blockchains are touted for their transparency; if you know someone's public key, you can look up all their transactions.

Data within smart contracts themselves are encoded but not encrypted. Encryption is used only to hash large datasets and verify transaction senders and recipients. However, you can encrypt data yourself before putting it into an Ethereum smart contract, if you'd like to use the public Ethereum chains in a private manner.

As you'll see later, every Ethereum transaction leaves room for an extra payload of text labeled Input Data. Don't be tempted to store secret things here for safekeeping unless you plan to encrypt them. Even then, it is generally a bad idea to store strings such as passwords or account pin numbers on the Ethereum blockchain because it is public and can never be removed. Anyone can explore a blockchain such as Ethereum by using a web-accessible application known as a *blockchain explorer*.

Blockchain Explorers

As with Bitcoin, every transaction in and out of the EVM is recorded publicly. The transaction shown in Figure 2-10 is a typical one for the Ethereum blockchain. Clicking the sender or recipient address allows you to see the transactions for that address since it was created. This screen capture is from Etherscan (`https://etherscan.io`), but anyone is free to make a blockchain explorer for the public Ethereum chain.

■ **Note** Blockchain explorers show you a historical record of all transactions in the network, and allow you to string together a history of transactions. There's no need to manually record your transaction details!

As you can see in Figure 2-10, transactions have quite a few attributes. We'll talk more about what these fields mean in Chapter 3, but for now here's the takeaway: sending and receiving ether is *private* to the participants and anyone they tell, because public keys

---

[4]Science Magazine, "Why Criminals Can't Hide Behind Bitcoin," `www.sciencemag.org/news/2016/03/why-criminals-cant-hide-behind-bitcoin`, 2016.

are pseudonymous by nature—but these transactions are not strictly *secret,* in the sense that all transactions are publicly viewable on the blockchain. It's easy to trace money hopping from one account to another.

Overview	
Transaction Information	
TxHash:	0xec9867d99e413e86a1106194f4add36780615a04719323822c750fcdb936301a
Block Height:	2385305 (1 block confirmation)
TimeStamp :	26 secs ago (Oct-05-2016 03:59:18 PM +UTC)
From:	0x9e6316f44baeeee5d41a1070516cc5fa47baf227 (Shapeshift2)
To:	0x491115fd45f4974f5c8cea3de396c5b6f63ea314
Value:	68.958894 Ether ($915.77)
Gas:	250000
Gas Price:	0.000000022787139656 Ether
Gas Used By Transaction:	21000
Actual Tx Cost/Fee:	0.00047852993277 Ether ($0.0064)
Cumulative Gas Used:	490472
Nonce:	59821
Input Data:	0x

Figure 2-10. All ether and bitcoin transactions are public. Some users avoid having their public key linked to their identity by creating a new account for every transaction. Others use the same public key for years, advertising it as a conduit for donations or contributions of one kind of another.

Summary

So far we've moved quickly. In this chapter, you learned more about wallets and Ethereum clients. If you began synchronizing your instance of Mist as you were reading this chapter, it's probably not even finished yet!

In the meantime, let's get prepared for deploying a smart contract.

Although you won't need access to an Ubuntu machine for the next chapter, it's worth lining up for Chapters 4, 5, 8, and 9. In the meantime, move on to the next chapter, where you'll learn how the Ethereum Virtual Machine works.

CHAPTER 3

The EVM

The Ethereum Virtual Machine (EVM) is a worldwide computer that anyone can use, for a small fee, payable in ether

The EVM is a single, global 256-bit "computer" in which all transactions are local on each node of the network, and executed in relative synchrony. It's a globally accessible virtual machine, composed of lots of smaller computers.

This giant computer, which anyone who has a node or wallet application can access, makes it simple to move arbitrarily large amounts of value (money) nearly instantly. Although anyone can use this global virtual machine, nobody can create counterfeit money inside it, or move funds without permission.

If it seems wasteful to have the entire EVM, all those nodes, replicating the same transactions and slavishly maintaining the same state among thousands of individual computers, it's important to have a proper basis for comparison for how financial services IT works today. The EVM is a paragon of simplicity and efficiency by comparison! More importantly, all that work isn't for naught. In fact, as you'll see in this chapter, it's the evidence of this work that actually secures the network.

The Central Bank Network of Yesterday

Today, corporations, insurers, universities, and other large institutions spend incredible amounts of money building and maintaining software services and IT for their own employees, and all their lines of business. Their various inflows and outflows are reconciled by large commercial banks, which have their own architecture, policy, codebase, databases, and layers of infrastructure. This, of course, is all *on top* of the Fedwire, which is the Federal Reserve's *real-time gross settlement system*, or RTGS.

The Federal Reserve is the central bank of the United States. The Fedwire is used by all Federal Reserve member banks to settle final payments in electronic US dollars. Any qualified state-chartered bank may become a member of the system by buying shares in it. Fedwire is owned and operated by the 12 Federal Reserve Banks themselves, and although it does charge fees, it isn't operated for profit.

This system processes unthinkable amounts of US dollars every day—trillions upon trillions. It has some great features, too: there's an overdraft system covering all

© Chris Dannen 2017
C. Dannen, *Introducing Ethereum and Solidity*, DOI 10.1007/978-1-4842-2535-6_3

existing and approved accounts, and the system is famously reliable, even for remittances overseas. It has been in operation in some form or another for about 100 years.

As you can imagine, maintaining the security and reliability of the Fedwire software is extremely expensive. Yet, the cost of building and maintaining layers on top of an RTGS is higher still, owing to its security requirements. Ultimately, these costs are passed on to corporations who use commercial banks, in the form of fees. Those companies have their own IT infrastructure costs. In the aggregate these costs ultimately drive up prices and fees for consumers.

What are Virtual Machines, Exactly?

If you were unfamiliar with virtual machines at the outset of this book, you've probably gathered by now that a virtual machine (VM), in the Ethereum context, is one giant global computer composed of constituent nodes, which are themselves computers too.

Generally speaking, a virtual machine is an *emulation* of a computer system by another computer system. These emulations are based on the same computer architectures as the target of their emulation, but they're usually reproducing that architecture on different hardware than it may have been intended for. Virtual machines can be created with hardware, software, or both. In the case of Ethereum, it's both. Rather than securely network thousands of discrete machines, as with Fedwire, Ethereum takes the approach of securely operating one very large machine that can encompass the whole Earth.

As you'll see from the long list of Ethereum clients for various operating systems, the EVM is a collective emulation being run on thousands of machines that—on an individual level—may be running any one of dozens of versions of Windows, Linux, ethOS, and macOS (more about ethOS in Chapter 6).

The Role of the Ethereum Protocol in Banking

It's beyond the scope of this book to posit whether blockchain-based systems are appropriate for use by, or are indeed the replacement for, sovereign central banks. It's much more likely that central banks themselves will adopt the technology. The commerical banks are certainly interested; you'll find more information about the banks and enterprises involved in Ethereum development in Chapter 11.

The Fedwire system is a settlement system with a user experience tailored to state-chartered banks and their operators. It makes little or no concern for the end user of a retail bank, for example; that's the job of the retail bank.

Software developers will recognize Fedwire as a "platform for banks." What the bank chooses to build on top of Fedwire (the customer experience, the online banking tools, the brick-and-mortar branches, the financial products, the cross-selling) is what distinguishes it from other banks on the Fedwire system.

Anyone Can Make a Banking Platform

Ethereum is far more generalized. It allows anyone to spin up a network with as good or better security and reliability than Fedwire, and with the ability to make secure value transfers nearly instantly. But this is only where Ethereum starts. Developers can build any sort of financial products or business logic they want on top of this secure ledger, with automated and immutable scripts, and without needing to pay the overheads dumped on them by the traditional centralized hosting and banking infrastructure.

But does it scale to the speed and size of a system like Fedwire? The answer is, yes, it can, but this will take several years. There are no direct or fixed limit neither for transaction sizes or block sizes. In Bitcoin, the size of the block is limited to 1MB, which works out to about 7 transactions per second. In Ethereum these limits increase and decrease in accordance with demand and network capacity.

However, this does not mean that blocks can be unlimited size. Recall that units of work in the Ethereum network are priced in gas. Thus, larger, more complex smart contracts cost more gas to store and execute. The maximum amount of gas which can be spent per block is variable, but there is a maximum. Theoretically, one large transaction could consume the entire gas limit of a single block. But if there is continuous demand for higher gas limits, the system will increase the gas limit per block in increments of 0.09 percent. (For more detail on how this works, see the Ethereum Yellow Paper, equations 40-42.) As of this writing, the gas limit is 4,041,325 gas per block.

What does this mean for the financial services industry? Certainly not doom, but perhaps some unexpected competition. The impact could be an unbundling of banking services into ever smaller brands as the public Ethereum chain scales and is capable of processing more transactions, faster and faster. Laura Shin, author and host of the blockchain-centric podcast Unchained, interviewed Adam Ludwin of San Francisco blockchain startup Chain in 2016 and wrote this:

> As for who owns the network, in the current system, if you go to Chase to deposit $50 cash, Chase holds that money, which was issued by the Federal Reserve, on its network. But Ludwin said you could imagine, instead of banks running the network, Fedwire, the current system for electronically settling payments between member banks, being reconstructed on a blockchain for which banks hold keys to make transfers.
>
> That could then lead to nonfinancial institutions being custodians of such currency. "With small enough amounts, you don't need a bank," said Ludwin. "Could Google, could Apple, could Facebook be holding small amounts of digital cash? Does that change the model of who a custodian is or could be? And the answer is yes." It could also open up more avenues for peer-to-peer lending, reducing consumers' reliance on banks for loans.[1]

What the EVM Does

By now, the EVM may be coming into focus: a generalized, secure, ownerless virtual machine that offers cheap Fedwire-like functionality with a bunch of other magic on top. How exactly does it do this?

---

[1]Forbes, "Central Banks Explore Blockchains: Why Digital Dollars, Pounds Or Yuan Could Be A Reality In 5 Years," `www.forbes.com/sites/laurashin/2016/10/12/central-banks-explore-blockchains-why-digital-dollars-pounds-or-yuan-could-be-a-reality-in-5-years/#5ef54e7176d8`, 2016.

The EVM can run arbitrary computer programs (the smart contracts mentioned in Chapter 1) written in the Solidity language. These programs, given a particular input, will always produce the output the same way, with the same underlying state changes. This makes Solidity programs fully *deterministic* and guaranteed to execute, provided you've paid enough for the transaction; but we'll talk about paying for gas later in this chapter.

Solidity programs are capable of expressing all tasks accomplishable by computers, making them theoretically *Turing complete*. That means that the entire distributed network, every node, performs every program executed on the platform. When one user uploads a smart contract through their Ethereum node, it is included in the latest block and propagated around the network, where it is stored on every other node in the network.

As we've discussed already, it's the job of each and every node in the EVM to run the same code, as part of the block processing protocol. The nodes go through the block they are process and run any code enclosed within the transactions. Each node does this independently; it is not only highly parallelized, but highly redundant.

Despite all appearances, this is an efficient way to balance a global ledger in a trustworthy way. It's important to remember just how much money, power, and human energy is spent for each bank everywhere to cobble together its own unique IT system or cocktail of systems for each of its lines of business. In an Ethereum-based banking system, all users (whether corporations or customers) get direct access to the same Fedwire-like system at no cost, with the ability to program transactions. Because the protocol is free and open source, anyone can fire up a node and connect. Unfortunately, the preceding explanation of the Fedwire system is often left out of cryptocurrency discussions, despite being necessary context to understanding the benefits of large public blockchains.

You can find up-to-date community-written documentation for the Ethereum project in the Homestead Documentation Initiative (`www.ethdocs.org/en/latest`). These docs are not endorsed by the Ethereum Foundation, but have grown into a popular resource for their plain-language explanation of technical concepts.

For more-nuanced technical discussions and to view Ethereum Improvement Proposals (EIPs), turn to the Ethereum wiki at `https://github.com/ethereum/wiki/wiki`. On the wiki, you'll find the Ethereum White Paper. If you have remaining questions about the way Ethereum works after reading this book, chances are the answer you seek is in the White Paper or the aforementioned Yellow Paper, which you'll also find linked on the Ethereum wiki.

Chapter 11 provides an additional index of academic papers associated with the Ethereum project. These relate to the future of the project, including scalability and interoperability of the Ethereum public chain with private or corporate chains, among other topics.

GLOBAL SINGLETON MACHINE

The EVM is a *transaction singleton machine with shared state*. In computing, this means it behaves like one giant data object, rather than what it is: a network of discrete machines, themselves singletons, in constant communication. (If you're a nonprogrammer, you may remember from Chapter 1 that an object is a little chunk of information that is formatted just so, and that contains attributes as well as methods for reading or changing those attributes.)

EVM Applications Are Called Smart Contracts

From the perspective of a software developer, the EVM is also a runtime environment for small programs that can be executed by the network.

The Name "Smart Contracts"

Rather than bore you with the etymology of this word, let's clear up one thing: in this context, *contract* refers to a specific kind of contract: a financial contract, also known more colloquially as a *derivative*, or *option*. Financial contracts are agreements to buy and sell at some point in the future, usually at a specified price. In the Ethereum context, smart contracts are agreements between accounts, to render a transfer of ether (that is, a payment) when certain conditions are met.

The reason these contracts are "smart" is that they're executed by machine, and the assets (ether or other tokens) are moved automatically. These contracts could be enforced even hundreds of years after they've been written, assuming the network is still running then—and even if a lot of bad actors try to interfere. The EVM is totally sandboxed and free from interference, and isolated from other networks too, making it impossible for a party to back out of a smart contract. In practical terms, this is because smart contracts are empowered to hold assets (ether or other tokens) in escrow and move them when the terms of the contract are met.

The EVM Runs Bytecode

The EVM has its own language, the *EVM bytecode*, to which your smart contracts compile. Solidity, which is a high-level language, is compiled into bytecode and uploaded onto the Ethereum blockchain by using a client application such as the Mist browser or a full node.

Understanding State Machines

The EVM, as we've discussed several times so far, is a *state machine*. Instead of simply defining this concept and moving on, let's take a moment to discuss *exactly what a computer is* before moving on to the ways that Ethereum advances the concept.

Digital vs. Analog

Foundational to the concept of a stateful computer is the idea of a switch that can be on or off. The 1s and 0s always referred to as the *lingua franca* of machines refer to arrays of metaphorical switches, so to speak, put in a certain configuration in order to code for specific letters, numbers, or other keyboard symbols. All of the symbols on a keyboard (and more) can be represented with just eight switches, which is why computing memory is stacked in multiples of eight. The so-called *character code* for a comma, for example, is 0010 1100.

In computer programming, letters and numbers can be used to write machine instructions colloquially known as *code*. American researcher and US Navy Rear Admiral Grace Hopper, shown in Figure 3-1, invented the first *compiler*, which automatically turned human-readable code into machine code (like the EVM's bytecode), which is less abstract and therefore one step closer to the 1s and 0s we hear so much about.[2]

Figure 3-1. *Rear Admiral Grace Hopper was one of the first programmers to write code for Harvard's Mark I computer in 1944. (Credit: Wikipedia.)*

"State-ments"

Individual snippets of code, when considered by themselves, fall broadly into two buckets: expressions and statements. *Expressions* are used to evaluate a particular condition; *statements* (note the root word!) are used to write information into the computer's memory. Together, expressions and statements let computers modify a database in a predictable way when specific conditions are met. This is the crux of automation, and it's the reason we find computers so useful!

Statements can evaluate to true or false, and depending on the code, this binary outcome can result in information being added, removed, or altered within one of the computer's many, many memory addresses. (Because the Solidity language is *strongly typed*, there are no "truthy" and "falsey" statements as in JavaScript.) The clear distinction between true and false, yes and no, on and off, is what allows computers to safely make decisions in lieu of humans.

---

[2]Wikipedia, "Grace Hopper," https://en.wikipedia.org/wiki/Grace_Hopper, 2016.

Data's Role in State

Every time you change data in a computer's memory, you can think of its zillions of internal switches (most of them virtualized in the same way we discussed earlier in this chapter) as being in a slightly different configuration. *State* generally refers to the present condition of the system: the objective series of changes in information, across various memory addresses of the machine, that led to the current contents of its memory.

It's important to distinguish between an attribute and state. State is something that can change easily and predictably. Let's use the example of a car.

Repainting a car is hard work, but it can be done. Paint color is an example of an attribute. In pseudocode, you might say the following about a car:

```
bodyColor = red
```

In computer programming, this is called a *key/value pair*. The key, bodyColor, has a value assigned to it, which is red. To change the value of this key, your code makes a new statement of the value to be something else:

```
bodyColor = green
```

And now your car has been repainted. It has a new color value.

Now let's say you instruct the computer that the color of this car will change frequently. In other words, you make the car's color a *variable*. Well, it can be said that the variable (in this case, the color) can have a state, which is a value that changes. But an individual value, such as green, has no state; green is simply green.

An odometer provides another example of a variable with a changeable state. The odometer's value might be 1,000, a number that itself has no state; it's just a number. Soon, the state of the odometer will change to a new value (1,001), but that will happen only if the cockpit of the car *expresses* commands that cause the motor and transmission to change state from *neutral* to *first gear*, and so on.

Working familiarity with the concept of state transition will help nonprogrammers gain insight into the truly hard problems incumbent in the design of decentralized systems. The next several sections of this chapter provide a crash course.

How the Guts of the EVM Work

If this is your first encounter with the internals of a computer, it's important to remember that a computer is never truly "at rest" as long as it's powered on. The computer itself is running a state function, constantly checking for changes to its state. It's like an overeager intern who wonders thousands of times per second if any new work has landed on his desk.

When new instructions are triggered, the computer runs code and may write new data to its memory. It's important to note that each state change must be based on the last state change; a computer doesn't just toss information into memory addresses willy-nilly.

Should something go wrong—let's say one of these instructions isn't mathematically possible—the state of the machine will become *invalid*, and the program will exit or stop. In fact, the entire system may crash.

Programs that constantly check for a certain condition are known as *loops* in programming, because they continue to run (to loop) until the specified condition is met. The EVM runs a loop continuously that attempts to execute whatever instructions are at the current program counter (whatever program is "on deck" to be processed). The program counter works like a delicatessen queue: each program takes a number and waits its turn.

This loop has a few jobs: it calculates the cost of gas for each instruction; and it uses memory, if necessary, to execute the transaction if the preamble calculation succeeds. This loop repeats until the VM either finishes running all the code on deck, or it throws an exception, or error, and that transaction is rolled back.

Thus far we've walked breezily through a century of computer science just to catch up to the EVM. Now we'll begin to slow down and see how some of the parts work in action.

The EVM Constantly Checks for Transactions

State machines (machines with memory) can be thought of as beings who never sleep. As a state machine, the EVM has a constant history of all transactions within their memory banks, leading all the way back to the very first transaction. Unlike people, who have to deal with imperfect memory, a computer's state (as it exists today) is the specific outcome of every single state-change that has taken place inside that machine since it was first switched on.

The latest version of the machine's state can be said to be this machine's canonical "truth" about reality as it stands right now. In Ethereum, this truth deals with account balances, and the series of transactions that make your balance whatever it is today.

Creating a Common Machine Narrative of What Happened

Transactions, therefore, represent a kind of machine narrative—a *computationally valid* arc between one state and another. As Gavin Wood's Ethereum Yellow Paper says:

> *There exist far more invalid state changes than valid state changes. Invalid state changes might, e.g., be things such as reducing an account balance without an equal and opposite increase elsewhere. A valid state transition is one which comes about through a transaction.*[3]

As time advances, the system (as in Bitcoin) seeks to create a trustworthy history for ensuring that each subsequent state change is legitimate, and not an instruction inserted by a bad actor.

---

[3]Gavwood.com, "Ethereum: A Secure Decentralised Generalised Transaction Ledger", http://gavwood.com/paper.pdf, 2016.

Cryptographic Hashing

The next section explains blocks: what's in them, how they work, and how they make a chain. To properly understand that discussion, you first need to learn about cryptographic hashing algorithms and what they're good for.

What Hash Functions (or Hash Algorithms) Do

Generally speaking, the purpose of hash functions, in the context of a blockchain, is to compare large datasets quickly and evaluate whether their contents are similar. A one-way algorithm processes the entire block's transactions into 32 bytes of data—a *hash*, or string, of letters and numbers that contains no discernible information about the transactions within. The hash creates an unmistakable signature for a block, allowing the next block to build on top of it. Unlike the *ciphertext* that results from encryption, which can be decrypted, the result of a hash cannot be "un-hashed."

▓ **Note**   The hash of a given dataset is always the same. It is computationally infeasible that two datasets might resolve to similar hashes. Changing even one character of the dataset will completely jumble up the hash.

Blocks: The History of State Changes

Transactions and state changes in the Ethereum network are segmented into blocks, and then hashed. Each block is verified and validated before the next canonical block can be placed on "top" of it. In this way, nodes on the network do not need to individually evaluate the trustworthiness of every single block in the history of the Ethereum network, simply to compute the present balances of the accounts on the network. They merely verify that its "parent block" is the most recent canonical block. They do this quickly by looking to see that the new block contains the correct hash of its parent's transactions and state.

All the blocks strung together, and including the *genesis block*, an honorific describing the first block the network mined after coming online, are called the *blockchain*. In some circles, you will hear the blockchain referred to as a *distributed ledger* or distributed ledger technology (DLT).

Ledger is an accurate description, as the chain contains every transaction in the history of the network, making it effectively a giant, balanced book of accounts. However, most so-called digital ledgers do not use proof of work to secure the network, as Bitcoin and Ethereum do.

Understanding Block Time

In Bitcoin, a block is 10 minutes. This so-called *block time* is derived from constants hard-coded into Bitcoin's issuance scheme, with a total of 21 million coins to be released from 2009 to 2024, and rewards halving every four years.[4]

In Ethereum, block time is not a function of the issuance schedule of ether. Instead, block time is a variable that is kept as low as possible, for the sake of speedy transaction confirmation. It averages about 15 seconds as of this writing. Ethereum's shorter block time is the beneficiary of blockchain research done after the launch of Bitcoin, which showed that shorter block times were not only technically feasible, but desirable in many ways. However, shorter block times do have some drawbacks that are explored more thoroughly in Chapter 6.

The Drawbacks of Short Blocks

It's important to note that Bitcoin's long confirmation times make retail commerce and other practical applications difficult. When blocks are shorter and transactions move faster, user experience is better. However, shorter blocks and faster transactions make it more likely that a given node will get the order of transactions wrong, because it may not have heard about some transactions originating from far away (or heard about them late).

To compensate for this, the miners who find blocks that are valid, but nonetheless not the winning block, are paid a reduced fee as consolation. In Ethereum, these blocks are called *Uncles*.

What makes a block *valid* vs. the *winner* is the subject of Chapter 6.

To see the full Ethereum block protocol, visit `https://github.com/ethereum/wiki/wiki/Block-Protocol-2.0`.

For now, let's continue with our overview of the EVM.

"Solo Node" Blockchain

In theory, you could reconcile changes from many nodes with a single computer: a centralized server processing the order of transactions. Indeed, web applications such as Google Docs have sophisticated real-time engines that help them deal with conflicting changes made by multiple users, some of whom may be on faster connections than others, and still others who may be editing a document offline.

As you'll see when you spin up your own blockchain in Chapter 9, it's possible to use the Ethereum protocol with a single machine. It will process your transactions just fine, as long as one or more nodes are mining on the chain. But if someone knocks that machine offline, your chain is inaccessible, and transactions stop going through.

For this reason, despite Ethereum being free and open software, the necessity for many, many nodes to create a resilient network causes developers to converge and work (for the most part) as one community, on a small number of public chains.

---

[4]Bitcoin Wiki, "Controlled Supply," `https://en.bitcoin.it/wiki/Controlled_supply`, 2016.

Distributed Security

The distributed nature of the Ethereum Virtual Machine, and the fact that it is composed of many nodes around the world, means that it must be purpose-built to solve the *diff-matching* problem that can arise when there are many near-simultaneous changes to the same database, from many users, all over the world.[5]

Indeed, solving this problem in a verifiable and trustworthy way is the purpose of the EVM as well as the Bitcoin virtual machine. The EVM's resilience and security arise from the large number of machines mining on the network, incentivized by the earning of fees denominated in ether or bitcoins. We'll go over this briefly before diving into a full explanation in Chapter 6.

Mining's Place in the State Transition Function

Mining is the process of using computational work to nominate a block—that miner's version of recent transaction history—as the canonical block for this, the most recent block on the chain. How exactly this happens is the subject of Chapter 6, but the point of bringing it up now is to show that mining incentive awards take place as part of the state-transition function. Mining achieves the consensus required to make valid state changes, and the miners are paid for contributing to the consensus building. This is how ether and bitcoin are "created."

Recall that each time a new block is created, it is downloaded, processed, and validated by node on the network. During processing, each node executes all the transactions contained therein. This is a long process with many steps, but we'll summarize. Written out in English, the Ethereum state transition function can be defined as the following six steps.[6] For each transaction in a block, the EVM performs the following:

1. Check whether the transaction is in the right format. Does it have the right number of values? Is the signature valid? Does the *nonce*—a transaction counter—on the transaction match the nonce on the account? If any of these are missing, return an error.

2. Calculate the transaction fee by multiplying the amount of work required (represented by STARTGAS, as you'll see in table 3-1) by the gas price. Then deduct the fee from the user's account balance, and increment the sender's nonce (transaction counter). If there's not enough ether in the account, return an error.

3. Initialize the gas payment; from this point forward, take off a certain amount of gas per byte processed in the transaction.

---

[5]Google Code, "Diff-Match Patch," https://code.google.com/p/google-diff-match-patch/, 2016.
[6]Ethereum White Paper, "Ethereum State Transition Function," https://github.com/ethereum/wiki/wiki/White-Paper#ethereum-state-transition-function, 2016.

4. Transfer the value of the transaction—the amount being sent—to the receiving account.

    If the receiving account doesn't exist yet, it will be created. (Offline Ethereum nodes can generate addresses, so the network may not hear of a given address until a transaction takes place.)

    If the receiving address is a contract address, run the contract's code. This continues either until the code finishes executing or the gas payment runs out.

5. If the sending account doesn't have enough ether to complete the transaction, or the gas runs out, all changes from this transaction are rolled back. A caveat are the fees, which still go to the miner and are not refunded.

6. If the transaction throws an error for any other reason, refund the gas to the sender and send any fees associated with gas used to the miner.

■ **Note**   Smart contract data is executed in Step 4 of the state transition function, as described above.

Renting Time on the EVM

As you may be gathering, the EVM is a rather deliberate machine, albeit far more trustworthy and reliable than any network we have today. For every instruction the EVM executes, there must be a cost associated, to ensure the system isn't jammed up by useless spam contracts.

Every time an instruction executes, an internal counter keeps track of the fees incurred, which are charged to the user. Each time the user initiates a transaction, that user's wallet reserves a small portion (selected by the user) to pay these fees.

After a transaction has been broadcast to the network from a given node—let's say Bob sends Alice some ether from his computer—the network propagates the transaction around so that all the nodes can include it in the latest block.

Believe it or not, the explanation so far in this chapter barely scrapes the surface of the EVM's internals. You'll learn more in Chapters 5 and 6. For now, it will be useful to break down the fees, their role in transaction execution, and their impact on development patterns.

Hello, Gas

Gas is a unit of work used to measure how computationally expensive an Ethereum operation will be. Gas costs are paid with small amounts of ether.

The purpose of gas is twofold. First, it guarantees a prepaid reward for the miners that execute code and secure the network, even if the execution fails for some reason. Second, it works around the *halting problem* and ensures that execution can't go on longer than the time it prepaid for.

Gas is a unit of work; it's not a subcurrency, and you can't hold or hoard it. It simply measures how much effort each step of a transaction will be, in computational terms.

To be able to pay for gas costs, you simply need to add ether to your account. You don't have to acquire it separately; there is no gas token. Every operation possible on the EVM has an associated gas cost.

▓ **Note**   It's the combination of total gas used multiplied by gas price paid that results in the total fee accrued by a given transaction.

Why Is Gas So Important?

Gas costs ensure that computation time on the network is appropriately priced. This works differently in Bitcoin, where the fee is based on the size of the transaction in kilobytes. Because Solidity code can be arbitrarily complex, a short snippet of instructions could generate a lot of computational work, whereas a long snippet could generate less. That's why fees in the EVM are based on the amount of work being done, not on the size of the transaction.

Why Isn't Gas Priced in Ether?

Because ether is traded publicly on cryptocurrency exchanges, it is subject to speculative periods of inflation and deflation. Using the gas unit of account for computational work is helpful because it separates the price of computation from the highly volatile price of the ether token.

Fees as Regulation

As you'll see in Chapter 7, networks such as Bitcoin and Ethereum use economic incentives and disincentives to render certain attack vectors moot. Fees fall into the category of disincentive.

To begin with, it's important to recognize that the operation of an Ethereum node represents some risk. There's the cost of the hardware, plus the time and energy of the operator, and the network's cost of downloading and verifying the proof of work and the block header. Thus it makes sense that a transaction fee be put in place to prevent pranksters from wasting the network's capacity.

Blocks that consume excessive amounts of gas are a big danger in Ethereum. They can take a long time to propagate because of their sheer size. How the system adapts to the demands of users, who may have legitimate uses for large smart contracts, will become clear later on in this chapter, and in Chapter 6. The protocol helps cut off late blocks using various methodologies we'll explore in Chapter 6, and places a floating cap on operations, which currently sits at 65,536 per block.[7]

Working with Gas

In this section, you'll explore the details of working with gas and then see how gas relates to scaling the system.

Gas Specifics

Let's review some details about working with gas:

- Unfortunately, the term *gas* creates some confusion. Every transaction requires a STARTGAS value. This value is referred to as gasLimit in the Yellow Paper and often just as gas in Geth and Web3.js.

- Every transaction also requires the user to specify a gas price.

- The amount stipulated in STARTGAS, multiplied by the gas price, is held in escrow while your transaction executes.

- If the gas price you offer for a transaction is too low, nodes won't process your transaction, and it will sit unprocessed on the network.

- If your gas price is acceptable to the network, but the gas cost runs over what's available in your wallet balance, the transaction fails and is rolled back; this failed transaction is recorded to the blockchain, and you get a refund of any STARTGAS not used in the transaction.

- Using excessive STARTGAS does not cause your transactions to be processed more quickly, and in some cases may make your transaction less appealing to miners.[8]

How Gas Relates to Scaling the System

If you send a computationally difficult set of instructions to the EVM, the only person this hurts is you. The work will spend your ether, and stop when the ether you allocated to the transaction runs out. It has no effect on anyone else's transactions. There is no way to jam up the EVM without paying a lot, in the form of transaction fees, to do it.

Scaling is handled in a de facto way through the gas fee system. Miners are free to choose the transactions that pay the highest fee rates, and can also choose the block gas limit collectively. The gas limit determines how much computation can happen (and how much storage can be allocated) per block.

---

[7]GitHub, "Ethereum White Paper," https://github.com/ethereum/wiki/wiki/White-Paper, 2016.
[8]ConsenSys Media, "Ethereum, Gas, Fuel and Fees," https://media.consensys.net/ethereum-gas-fuel-and-fees-3333e17fe1dc#.ozbhydyz6, 2016.

In this way, the price of computation on the EVM stays flexible and responsive to the demand of the users of the system, as well as the costs incurred by the miners who do the important work of processing transactions, maintaining hardware, and paying electricity bills.

Accounts, Transactions, and Messages

Recall from Chapter 2 that Ethereum has two types of accounts:

Externally owned accounts

Contracts accounts

Let's look more deeply into exactly what each account type can do.

Externally Owned Accounts

An *externally owned account* (EOA) is also known as an account controlled by a pair of private keys, which may be held by a person or an external server. These accounts cannot hold EVM code. Characteristics of an EOA include the following:

- Contains a balance of ether

- Capable of sending transactions

- Controlled by the account's private keys

- Has no code associated with it

- A key/value database contained in each account, where keys and values are both 32-byte strings

Contract Accounts

Contract accounts are not controlled by humans. They store instructions and are activated by external accounts or other contract accounts. Contract accounts have the following characteristics:

- Have an ether balance

- Hold some contract code in memory

- Can be triggered by humans (sending a transaction) or other contracts sending a message

- When executed, can perform complex operations

- Have their own persistent state and can call other contracts

- Have no owner after being released to the EVM

- A key/value database contained in each account, where keys and values are both 32-byte strings

Transactions and Messages

Transactions come from external accounts, which are usually controlled by human users. It's a way for an external account to submit instructions to the EVM to perform some operation. In other words, it's a way for an external account to get a message into the system. In computing terminology, a *message* is a chunk of data containing instructions. Programmers can think of messages as function calls.

A *transaction* in the EVM is a cryptographically signed data package storing a message (as described previously), which tells the EVM to transfer ether, create a new contract, trigger an existing one, or perform some calculation. Contract addresses can be the recipients of transactions, just like users with external accounts. Recall the discussion of cryptographic communication from Chapter 2, in which we discussed encrypted communications: a transaction is like a private communication between two users in an unsecured network, who are nevertheless able to "send" value to each other.

Characteristics of Transactions

Transactions contain the following:

- A recipient address; specifying no recipient (and attaching smart contract data) is the method for uploading new smart contracts. As you'll see, a contract address is returned so that the user knows where to access this contract in the future.

- A signature identifying the sender

- A value field showing the amount being sent

    - An optional data field, for a message (if this is being sent to a contract address)

- A STARTGAS value, indicating the maximum number of computational steps the transaction are prepaid

- A GASPRICE value, representing the fee the sender is willing to pay for gas

Characteristics of Messages

A *message* is a chunk of data sent by a contract to another contract (never to or from a human). Messages are virtual objects that are never serialized and exist only in the EVM. When a miner is paid in the Ethereum network, this is accomplished by way of a message to increment the miner's payment address; it does not constitute a transaction.

A message is sent when a contract is being run by the EVM, and it executes the CALL or DELEGATECALL opcodes. You will learn about opcodes in the next section of this chapter.

Messages are sent to other contract accounts, which in turn run the code enclosed in the message. Thus, contracts can have relationships with each other.

A message contains the following:

- The sender address of the message

- The recipient address of the message

- The value field (indicating how much ether, if any, is being sent)

- An optional data field (containing input data for the contract)

- A STARTGAS value limiting the amount of gas the message can use

Estimating Gas Fees for Operations

Transactions need to provide enough STARTGAS to cover all computation and storage. However, but there are many operations in the EVM, and it's hard to memorize what each one costs.

Table 3-1 shows the costs of some common EVM operations.

Table 3-1. Costs of Common EVM Operations

Operation Name	Gas Cost	Description
step	1	Default amount per execution cycle
stop	0	Free
suicide	0	Free
sha3	20	SHA-3 hash function
sload	20	Gets from permanent storage
sstore	100	Puts into permanent storage
balance	20	Queries account balance
create	100	Contract creation
call	20	Initiating a read-only call
memory	1	Every additional word when expanding memory
txdata	5	Every byte of data or code for a transaction
transaction	500	Base fee transaction
contract creation	53,000	Changed in homestead from 21,000

An up-to-date Google Doc containing the costs of various EVM operations can be found at http://gas.eth.guide.

Opcodes in the EVM

As you'll see, some of these operations can be called as methods. One of the most confusing things about the blockchain paradigm is that it combines technical conventions from several domains of computer science and networking. One example is Ethereum's (and Bitcoin's) use of *opcodes*, or operation codes. Table 3-2 shows all the opcodes available on the EVM, and their respective functions.

In traditional web development, the rough equivalent of an opcode would be a HTTP verb, also known as an HTTP method. These include GET, POST, HEAD, OPTIONS, PUT, DELETE, TRACE, and CONNECT. These semantics are reliable and well-known.

In Ethereum and Bitcoin, things work differently. Because the network is also a global machine, the "methods" you use to make calls across the network are just machine-language codes, of the ilk used inside an individual computer.

The following is a full list of EVM opcodes:

Table 3-2. *This is a complete list of EVM opcodes*

0s: Stop and Arithmetic Operations

0x00	STOP	Halts execution.
0x01	ADD	Addition operation.
0x02	MUL	Multiplication operation.
0x03	SUB	Subtraction operation.
0x04	DIV	Integer division operation.
0x05	SDIV	Signed integer.
0x06	MOD	Modulo.
0x07	SMOD	Signed modulo.
0x08	ADDMOD	Modulo.
0x09	MULMOD	Modulo.
0x0a	EXP	Exponential operation.
0x0b	SIGNEXTEND	Extend length of 2s (complement signed integer).

10s: Comparison and Bitwise Logic Operations

0x10	LT	Lesser-than comparison.
0x11	GT	Greater-than comparison.
0x12	SLT	Signed less-than comparison.
0x13	SGT	Signed greater-than comparison.
0x14	EQ	Equality comparison.

(continued)

Table 3-2. (*continued*)

0x15	ISZERO	Simple NOT operator.
0x16	AND	Bitwise AND operation.
0x17	OR	Bitwise OR operation.
0x18	XOR	Bitwise XOR operation.
0x19	NOT	Bitwise NOT operation.
0x1a	BYTE	Retrieve single byte from word.

20s: SHA3

0x20	SHA3	Compute Keccak-256 hash.

30s: Environmental Information

0x30	ADDRESS	Get address of currently executing account.
0x31	BALANCE	Get balance of the given account.
0x32	ORIGIN	Get execution origination address.
0x33	CALLER	Get caller address. This is the address of the account directly responsible for this execution.
0x34	CALLVALUE	Get deposited value by the instruction/transaction responsible for this execution.
0x35	CALLDATALOAD	Get input data of current environment.
0x36	CALLDATASIZE	Get size of input data in current environment.
0x37	CALLDATACOPY	Copy input data in current environment to memory. Pertains to the input data passed with the message call instruction or transaction.
0x38	CODESIZE	Get size of code running in current environment.
0x39	CODECOPY	Copy code running in current environment to memory.
0x3a	GASPRICE	Get price of gas in current environment.
0x3b	EXTCODESIZE	Get size of an account's code.
0x3c	EXTCODECOPY	Copy an account's code to memory.

40s: Block Information

0x40	BLOCKHASH	Get the hash of one of the 256 most recent complete blocks.
0x41	COINBASE	Get the block's beneficiary address.
0x42	TIMESTAMP	Get the block's timestamp.
0x43	NUMBER	Get the block's number.
0x44	DIFFICULTY	Get the block's difficulty.
0x45	GASLIMIT	Get the block's gas limit.

(*continued*)

Table 3-2. (*continued*)

50s: Stack, Memory, Storage, and Flow Operations

0x50	POP	Remove item from stack.
0x51	MLOAD	Load word from memory.
0x52	MSTORE	Save word to memory.
0x53	MSTORE8	Save byte to memory.
0x54	SLOAD	Load word from storage.
0x55	SSTORE	Save word to storage.
0x56	JUMP	Alter the program counter.
0x57	JUMPI	Conditionally alter the program counter.
0x58	PC	Get the value of the program counter prior to the increment.
0x59	MSIZE	Get the size of active memory in bytes.
0x5a	GAS	Get the amount of available gas, including the corresponding reduction.
0x5b	JUMPDEST	Mark a valid destination for jumps.

60s and 70s: Push Operations

0x60	PUSH1	Place 1-byte item on stack.
0x61	PUSH2	Place 2-byte item on stack.
0x7f	PUSH32	Place 32-byte (full word) item on stack.

80s: Duplication Operations

0x80	DUP1	Duplicate first stack item.
0x81	DUP2	Duplicate second stack item.
0x8f	DUP16	Duplicate 16th stack item.

90s: Exchange Operations

0x90	SWAP1	Exchange first and second stack items.
0x91	SWAP2	Exchange first and third stack items.
0x9f	SWAP16	Exchange 1st and 17th stack items.

a0s: Logging Operations

0xa0	LOG0	Append log record with no topics.
0xa1	LOG1	Append log record with one topic.
0xa4	LOG4	Append log record with four topics.

(*continued*)

Table 3-2. (*continued*)

f0s: System Operations

0xf0	CREATE	Create a new account with associated code.
0xf1	CALL	Message-call into an account.
0xf2	CALLCODE	Message-call into this account with alternative account's code.
0xf3	RETURN	Halt execution returning output data.
0xf4	DELEGATECALL	Message-call into this account with an alternative account's code, but persisting the current values for sender and value. Halt execution; mark for deletion.
0xff	SUICIDE	Halt execution and register account for later deletion.

Summary

This chapter has provided a more complete vision of the EVM as a database, and how changes are made to its state. Although the design rationale should be clearer to you now, there's still a lot left to discuss. If you'd like to read more ancillary documentation about how the EVM executes programs, you'll find a list of resources at http://evm.eth.guide.

The question to tackle next: what does it mean to *run programs* on the EVM? The answer lies in writing and deploying smart contracts, which work in concert to form *distributed applications*.

As we discussed in this chapter, each contract has its own address with storage, where it can hold any arbitrary code. When a transaction hits this address, or the contract is called by another contract, its code springs to life inside every node on the EVM, leading to further message passing or ether transactions.

The instructions that make up smart contracts are stored in EVM bytecode. But before they are compiled into bytecode, they are written by a human, in the Solidity programming language. That language is the subject of the next chapter.

CHAPTER 4

Solidity Programming

Solidity is a new programming language used to write programs called smart contracts, which can be run by the EVM. This new language is a hodgepodge of conventions from networking, assembly language, and web development

Imagine you're on a beach in another country. You took a trip here on a whim and breezed past the currency exchange booth in the airport, figuring you could use your credit or debit card while visiting—no need for cash. In your rush, you forgot to bring sunglasses. A vendor walking along the beach has a pair that happen to be your style. In fact, they're better than the pairs you remember passing in the duty-free area of the airport. Alas, he doesn't have a credit card reader—just his Android phone—and you don't have any local currency. He gives you a little card with an e-mail address and a phone number, in case you'd like to buy the glasses later.

Think about this scenario for a moment, and you'll see the power of protocol-based digital currency. Why can you send this man a text message or an e-mail, or even call him on the phone, but you can't send him money the same way?

Primer

The preceding chapter described how the EVM transitions state, and in this chapter you'll see what kind of instructions the EVM can process as it makes state transitions.

In general, a computing environment is an infinite loop that repeatedly carries out whatever operation is current in the system's program counter. (Jumping the queue in the program counter is where the JUMP opcodes derive their name.) The program counter iterates one by one until the end of that particular program is reached. The machine exits the execution loop only if it encounters (*throws*) an error, or hits an instruction designating the machine to STOP or RETURN a result or value.

© Chris Dannen 2017
C. Dannen, *Introducing Ethereum and Solidity*, DOI 10.1007/978-1-4842-2535-6_4

These operations have access to three types of space in which to store data:

> The *stack*, a container in which values can be added or removed (*pushed* or *popped*). Stack values are defined within a method.

> *Dynamic memory*, also known as *the heap*, an infinitely expandable byte array. This resets when the program finishes.

> A *key/value store* for account balances and, in the case of contract addresses, Solidity code.

Solidity contracts can also access certain attributes about the incoming message, such as the value, sender, and data of the incoming message, as well as the data from the block header.

Global Banking Made (Almost) Real

The banks of the world have computer systems that, while upgraded and mostly modern, are the descendants of machines that predate the Internet and certainly the World Wide Web. As a result, they're architected to be silos. There is no single global banking network, but rather an interconnected mass of national systems and private banking software stacks, all with their own quirks.

Extra-Large Infrastructure

A system such as Ethereum has nodes all over the world, being operated by private individuals who are paid for their activity in the form of mining fees, denominated in ether. How this works is the subject of Chapter 6. The system is highly decentralized.

As a result, cryptocurrency protocols have the power to elevate financial transactions to the level of convenience we now enjoy with our telecommunications. So, how does a decentralized system of peer-to-peer nodes run "programs," anyway?

Worldwide Currency?

As you can see, the idea of a universal cryptocurrency seems to rest on the assumption that every human on Earth will eventually download a cryptocurrency wallet onto their cell phone. However, such a pipe dream is not the roadmap for Ethereum. Instead, the Ethereum Core developers have chosen to make it easy for third parties to create *complementary currencies*, or custom tokens, that will be branded and used for special purposes (similar to credit card rewards points today). These third parties (whether existing corporations, startups, municipalities, universities, or nongovernmental organizations) could rely upon the public chain, or large permissioned chains, to push around many different types of tokens, much the way that the global banking system is equipped to handle many different currencies.

It's unlikely that most people's first experience with ether will be for the sake of cryptocurrency experimentation. It's more likely they will end up holding digital tokens or points as part of a brand loyalty program, university program, or employer-sponsored system. Sports stadiums, theme parks, city summer camps, shopping malls, large office parks—anywhere there's a community exchanging money, a complementary currency might make sense.

Complementary Currency

Why would a country ever need more than one form of money? In the decades leading up to the establishment of the Federal Reserve, the United States' present-day central bank, many local currencies circulated. These paper bills generally represented gold on deposit somewhere, and were thus local by nature; a certificate for gold is worth little if the redeeming institution is thousands of miles away. In the period before widespread, systematic private money systems (a period of American history known as the *Wildcat banking* era), many printing houses made their primary incomes from printing money with various anticounterfeiting features to rival their competing printing houses.

Benjamin Franklin was one such printer who enriched himself on the printing of complementary currencies. In fact, he was known for his anticounterfeiting measures that went above and beyond. According to the Smithsonian Institution, he once printed an official issuance of local Pennsylvania currency with the name of the state spelled wrong, in the hopes of foiling counterfeiters who assumed those bills must be fake.[1] Many of Franklin's colonial bills bore the words *to counterfeit is death.*[2]

The term *complementary currency* refers to a medium of exchange functioning alongside national fiat currency, meeting a need the national coin cannot. These currencies generally have four purposes[3]:

> To promote local economic development within a small community
>
> To build social capital in that community
>
> To nurture more-sustainable lifestyles
>
> To meet needs that mainstream money does not

Solidity programming allows anyone to create a complementary currency, with a simple token contract. Those tokens can have whatever parameters the situation calls for, as you'll see when you deploy a token contract in Chapter 5.

The Promise of Solidity

Solidity is a high-level contract-oriented language with similarities to JavaScript and C languages. It allows you to develop contracts and compile to EVM bytecode. It is currently the flagship language of Ethereum. Although it's the most popular language library to be written for the EVM, it was not the first and probably will not be the last.

---

[1]Smithsonian Education, "Revolutionary Money," http://www.smithsonianeducation.org/educators/lesson_plans/revolutionary_money/introduction.html, 2016.
[2]Wikipedia, "Counterfeit Money," https://en.wikipedia.org/wiki/Counterfeit_money, 2016.
[3]Investopedia, "Complementary Currency," www.investopedia.com/articles/economics/11/introduction-complementary-currencies.asp, 2016.

There are four languages in the Ethereum protocol at the same level of abstraction, but the community has slowly converged on Solidity, which has edged out Serpent (similar to Python), Lisp-Like Language (LLL), and Mutan, the latter of which is deprecated.

Learning Solidity enables you to move tokens of value in any Ethereum-based system. And because Ethereum and Solidity itself are free and open source technology, clever minds will likely alter and re-release it, or deploy it privately. In fact, several groups have already done just that; you'll learn about these third parties and their approaches in later Chapter 11.

You can find the official Solidity documentation at `http://solidity.readthedocs.io/en/develop/index.html`. However, other sites also offer useful Solidity docs. For convenience, all the most popular Solidity documentation is linked under the `http://solidity.eth.guide` subdomain.

Browser Compiler

The most common way to test Solidity is by using the browser-based compiler. It can be found at `http://ethereum.github.io/browser-solidity`. For quick reference, you'll also find it at `http://compiler.eth.guide`.

If you've read this far, you might already be curious about how to learn Solidity yourself. Although it's certainly easier to begin programming in Solidity if you already know another programming language, don't let this discourage you if you're a nonprogrammer.

Learning to Program the EVM

Sometimes it's easier to learn a new habit than to break an old one. Many conventions in distributed application programming will strike today's web and native application programmers as odd or quirky. Plus, they may already be professionally or personally invested in other languages or subject areas. So don't feel like the whole world has a head start on you if you're just starting out. It is still early days in the world of Ethereum.

■ **Note** Key programming terms will be defined as we go, and you'll pick up a lot from the context. Try looking through a JavaScript book aimed at beginners (`http://www.apress.com/us/book/9781484217863`) for a deeper explanation of some of the core concepts in this chapter.

New coders can approach Ethereum without preexisting assumptions. Better yet, they'll find a system they can (admittedly, after some time) understand from top to bottom. Not all hackers, nor even software engineers, know the intricacies of the underlying networks in the layers below their application hosting provider.

In conventional web applications, you have many individual servers with databases, communicating and sharing data over a network. This data may be manipulated by applications that live on still *other* servers. Even more servers may be in the mix to balance surges in demand.

> ■ **Note** A *server* is a computer that acts in a dedicated role, as part of a certain kind of service you want to offer people via the Web. Some servers hold data (think of spreadsheets of information, such as customer names and addresses) in what are known as *databases*. Some servers run applications that other computers can access over the network.

In Ethereum, the *network is the database*, and this network can run applications available to everyone on it. So you end up learning quite a bit about all three.

Watching a blockchain explorer report new transactions is something of a marvel when you know what's happening underneath. Although learning Ethereum may seem like a lot of work, it would be much more work to understand today's Web with a similar breadth and depth.

The following subsections present other reasons you should begin experimenting with Solidity.

Easy Deployment

In Ethereum, you don't necessarily have much of the hassle of deploying and scaling a normal web application. All the required smart contracts for the back-end of distributed app, also known as a *dapp,* can be neatly bundled up in a few documents and sent to the EVM, and boom—your program is available instantly to anyone on Earth who installs an Ethereum wallet or command-line node. Today, developers may want to build "hybrid" Ethereum dapps that are accessible through normal Web browsers, in which case adding ether payments is just adding more work. But by the time the network is complete in 2-3 years, it will be able to far easier to host all the components of an application using the Ethereum protocol.

> ■ **Note** In business jargon, *time to value*, or *TTV*, is the amount of time that passes from the moment the customer requests something to the moment the customer gets it. This *something* can be tangible or intangible. But a low TTV suggests that it is easy to think up a product or service and deliver it quickly to the people who want to use it.

In Ethereum, it is fast and inexpensive (if not yet easy) to develop and deploy unalterable, always-up, uncensorable applications that move real value over arbitrary distances. And everything is free, except the gas costs generated by your programs, and your own time (and computer). For software engineers, service providers, system administrators, and product managers, the long-term impact of working in the Ethereum ecosystem means less brittle systems, faster product iterations, and far less time developing infrastructure to support new applications or services. In short, this may amount to a drastic reduction in TTV for enterprise software vendors and in-house teams alike.

The Case for Writing Business Logic in Solidity

Because of its novel characteristics, the fate of Ethereum in 2017 and beyond doesn't necessarily rest on the mainstream popularity or adoption of today's Ethereum clients. Instead, it relies on popularity with developers, brands, corporations, organizations, governments, and other institutions that are in a position to create an Ethereum token for their community, and perhaps even their own branded wallet.

They might do so in the interest of quickly and safely rolling out cool new products and services with ultra-low overhead. This also goes for large marketing campaigns, which must be deployed faster and faster today to keep up with the speed of Internet meme culture. The frictionless nature of the payments in cryptonetworks makes it easier than ever to build a seamless sales and marketing experience for customers, with payments built in.

A complementary currency is also a highly valuable tool for use in rewards programs, membership clubs, and large retail districts. Customers who hold money in the form of a branded coin are apt to spend more regularly on that brand, just as frequent flyers today stay loyal to the airline miles and credit-card point schemes that give them the best bang for the buck.

Today, loyalty programs can be obscure and even slightly scammy. But the transparency of a blockchain-based loyalty coin would make it as good as any other form of cryptocurrency—meaning it might be traded on exchanges or accepted by other parties as payment.

Code, Deploy, Relax

Many Ethereum-enabled applications might be used through the Mist wallet, or another Ethereum-native application running a node under the hood. For developers of client applications, adding compatibility with new Ethereum-based tokens is trivial, meaning that a high degree of overlap and intercompatibility will exist between Ethereum wallets and tokens, just as there are many IMAP- and POP-compatible e-mail clients today.

It's also possible to create an Ethereum program today that is accessible through the regular old Web, with a little bit of work. However, deployment will be made increasingly easy with the use of new third-party frameworks, examples of which are provided in Chapter 8.

However, this isn't to say that conventional web apps will go away. Many individuals and organizations have enormous resources invested in legacy web apps. That said, the Ethereum network makes it far easier and cheaper to roll out and operate applications at large scale, as you'll see, tempting more and more teams to consider decentralizing their applications.

Design Rationale

The Solidity programming language has a syntax like JavaScript, but it is specially designed to compile into bytecode for the Ethereum Virtual Machine. As noted in Chapter 3, the EVM runs code that is fully deterministic; the same algorithms with the same inputs will always yield the same results. You can prove this mathematically, as you'll see later in this chapter.

Solidity is statically typed, supports inheritance, libraries, and complex user-defined types, among other features. Conscientious use of types can help programmers understand how their programs will execute. A list of types in Solidity is presented at the end of this chapter.

■ **Note**   *Data types* are exactly what they sound like. A programmer has the option of telling the machine what type of data to expect: for example, will it be a number or a string of letters? Loosely typed languages don't require the programmer to be specific; strongly typed languages do.

Interestingly, in Solidity you can write assembly code inline. If you prefer to do a certain operation by using one of the EVM's opcodes, listed in Chapter 3, you can do so inline in your Solidity contracts. Just write `assembly {...}` with your code in place of a Solidity statement.

Writing Loops in Solidity

Loops are foundational to control flow in programming—that is, the codification of if-this-then-that contingencies or do-this-while-doing-that concurrencies. In most programming languages, loops are initiated with similar syntax. Solidity adheres to all the same syntactical regularities as JavaScript and C when it comes to loops.

An *iterator* loop is an object that enables a programmer to move through a container or list. Sometimes, iterators are used to instruct the computer to perform the same operation a certain number of times, or on a number of elements in the code.

A general-purpose loop has the same syntax in JavaScript, C, and Solidity. It instructs the computer to count up from 0 to 10:

```
for (i = 0; i < 10; i++) {...}
```

If you looked carefully at the list of opcodes in the preceding chapter, you may have noticed that the EVM allows looping in two ways. You can write loops in Solidity, or you can create them using JUMP and JUMPI instructions. This jumps ahead a specified number of steps in the program counter. Recall that the program counter keeps track of the number and order of computational steps in a given program as it is being executed on the EVM.

This is just one way that Solidity and EVM opcodes can be used together to create a contract that is mostly expressive and readable, but also cheap to run. It's important to point out that because of the way gas price is calculated, some functionality might be easier to enforce or less expensive to execute if written using opcodes, and this can be especially useful if you're writing your own language library.

If you've never looked seriously at code before, and this loop concept is hard to grasp, don't sweat it now; the following sections provide more context.

Expressiveness and Security

The adjective *expressive* is used in computer science to mean code that is easy for a human programmer to write and to understand. Expressive languages are the bridge between human thought patterns and machine execution patterns. For a language to be expressive, its various constructs must be intuitively readable, and its boilerplate code (such as keywords, special variables, and opcodes) must use human-readable words that help programmers remember what they represent.

Expressive languages must be *compiled down* into something more machine-friendly before they can be run, and this requires work on the part of the computer. After all, expressive languages tend to be harder to reason about (harder to predict the behavior of), whereas more-restricted, lower-level, less-abstract languages make that reasoning easier.

The final frontier is smart contracts that can be easily formally verified, but also written in an expressive high-level language such as Solidity. This problem begs for automation, and indeed, automated formal verification is now on the horizon—a fact that computer scientists must be excited about, and that Ethereum developers will unknowingly benefit from.

The Importance of Formal Proofs

If you learn Solidity programming, you may encounter the curiosity of other developers, who will get right to the point: how do you prevent someone writing an infinite loop and locking up the machine?

Far from being a niche argument, this is the most relevant issue related to software engineering's role in the world today: *can human beings make a free, openly accessible virtual computer that other human beings can't sabotage?* If the answer is yes, then it stands in stark defiance of the theory of the tragedy of the commons.

Historical Impact of a Shared Global Resource

In economics, the *tragedy of the commons* is the idea that a shared resource can't last. Eventually, users acting in their own self-interests will deplete the resource, because it comes at no cost to themselves to do so. A scenario like this, whereby someone can enrich themselves or act profligately while externalizing the costs to other people, is known as a *moral hazard*.

Here's an example: In New York City in late 2016, the municipal government installed computing terminals on the streets of Lower Manhattan. These terminals offered free Wi-Fi to passing pedestrians. However, these terminals also came with a small touchscreen allowing walk-up Internet access. No sooner were these shared resources up and running before people were pulling up chairs, watching YouTube or pornography, and loitering for hours.[4] Program administrators were forced to quickly restrict the onscreen Internet access, and now the terminals serve mostly as just Wi-Fi hotspots.

---

[4]New York Times, "Internet Browsers to Be Disabled on New York's Free Wi-Fi Kiosks," `www.nytimes.com/2016/09/15/nyregion/internet-browsers-to-be-disabled-on-new-yorks-free-wi-fi-kiosks.html?_r=0`, 2016.

Thus, the notion of an extremely inexpensive public computer such as the EVM is nothing short of fantastic. It can be accessed by anyone, with any computer, anywhere, and will run programs far into the future. Nobody owns it and nobody can tamper with it. It can even store your money for you.

How Attackers Bring Down Communities

Decentralized economies represent a nascent threat to all sorts of private vested interests around the world, especially in developing economies, where powerful people would prefer the world continue on without a solution to the tragedy of the commons (and thus, remain at the mercy of the latest autocrat or crazy mob). The security of the Ethereum network is the subject of Chapter 7. But Ethereum's defenses are everywhere, even in the programming language itself, so it bears mention here.

For this discussion, you can think of a *network* as a community of people connecting with each other via computer. An *attacker* is someone who hates this group, and seeks to cause them grief at any expense.

Hypothetical Attack Written in Solidity

Imagine that an attacker wants to lock up the EVM with a super memory-intensive smart contract, written in Solidity. The attacker is willing to pay the gas costs, however large. (This is a real scenario, as you'll see in Chapter 7.) Keep in mind that for the purposes of this example, the contract could also be written in any language created for the EVM, such as Serpent or even the lower-level EVM code, not just Solidity.

According to Rice's theorem, the behavioral properties of some computer programs are mathematically undecidable, meaning it is not possible to write another computer program that can definitively predict whether Solidity code you show it will ever terminate.[5] Thus, there is no way to write any kind of effective "gatekeeper" program that will swat down a hypothetically memory-hungry smart contract written by the attacker in this scenario.

▓ **Note** Smart contracts are distinct from distributed applications, or dapps, even though both are distributed and application-like. A *dapp* is a GUI application that uses Ethereum smart contracts on the back end, in lieu of a conventional database and web application hosting provider. Dapps may be accessed through the Mist browser or over the Web.

The EVM deals with this reality in various ways, including a hard limit on the number of computational steps per block, its deterministic language, and gas costs. Nevertheless, gray areas will always be explored by attackers if a financial incentive exists, and at $1 billion market capitalization, there's significant incentive to crack the EVM and steal ether.

Although gray areas can't be engineered away at once, they can be dealt with in a series of protocol forks over time. As far as accidentally destructive programs, it's up

---

[5]Wikipedia, "Rice's Theorem," https://en.wikipedia.org/wiki/Rice%27s_theorem, 2016.

to the Ethereum community to develop patterns and practices that are conducive to straightforward, easy-to-prove contracts that can develop into boilerplate standards. Chapter 5 covers some of these best practices.

Automated Proofs to the Rescue?

Although it's not possible to create a gatekeeper that kicks out bad programs, it is increasingly feasible to produce provably correct programs by using a machine-checkable proof—an automated program that mathematically proves other programs.

Because smart contracts move money, they make great lab rats for automated mathematical proofs. The goal of this area of computer science and mathematics research is to ensure, in a systematic way, that source code satisfies a certain formal specification. It's a way for independent auditors to come in and mathematically verify that the program is actually doing what it's supposed to do.

Automating the proving process is a boon for businesses but won't do much for the average programmer learning Solidity. Proofs merely show you whether what you *intended* to happen actually *did* happen in the program. If your program doesn't prove out, there is no way for an automated system to tell you how to write it better.

Nevertheless, the point of exploring this topic is to signal that Ethereum networks may indeed one day carry high volumes of automated money-moving bots pushing around trillions of dollars safely; and that developing these bots may not be as slow, risky, and obscure a process as it is today.

Determinism in Practice

Combining the concepts from the preceding sections, you can see that in some ways, the whole idea of Turing completeness may be an idealized concept of limited usefulness when designing a public system in the real world.

Thus, it could also be said that in practice, the EVM is not really Turing complete, because the bounded nature of execution in Solidity contracts could soon make it possible to theoretically predict the behavior of any program the EVM will run.

Bitcoin escapes none of these issues. The gray areas that exist between expressive languages and machine languages exist for Bitcoin's scripting language too, which is also compiled down at runtime into machine code.

Lost in Translation

Interestingly, the question of proofs has a lot to do with the concept of *expressiveness*, discussed earlier in this chapter. A human can perform a mathematical proof on only a high-level, abstract language—that is, a human-readable programming language such as Solidity. Performing such a proof on assembly code or machine code would be next to impossible for even the most dedicated mathematical minds.

The compilation process—the transmission of human-readable code into lower-level machine code—sacrifices a lot of (human interpretable) information about how to reason about the program. It also sacrifices information that would be useful to an automated theorem prover. Thus, some ambiguity is always introduced into the process. Today, you can never be fully sure that even a mathematically proven smart contract written in Solidity will still be provable after being compiled.

Testing, Testing, Testing

The way to prevent ambiguous code from losing your money is to test vigorously. The Ethereum network comes with a testnet called *Ropsten* that uses play ether, which costs nothing and can be drawn from a faucet quickly in a sandbox-like environment.

In reality, Ropsten is no different from the main chain. It is simply a different chain that was designated for testing. Like the *Titanic* and its sister ship the *Britannic*, they are identical except for the names, as is every other chain someone spins up. There is nothing special or sanctified about these chains; you will create chains just like them in Chapter 8.

Command Line Optional!

Keep in mind that most of the important functions of Ethereum can be done in the Mist wallet: sending and receiving ether, tracking tokens, and deploying contracts. Using Geth (or the other command-line clients) is a good choice for developers who intend to learn to write dapps. Chapter 6 deals more with Geth.

In this section, we will look briefly at a real smart contract, to explore one simple example of how a smart contract can be used.

■ **Note** If you can't read or write code, don't worry. A tutorial on syntax and structure follows this example that will help you reason about what the code is doing. In the next chapter, we'll deploy a standard Ethereum token, with zero coding required.

You'll learn how to deploy a contract like this in Chapter 5. You'll be pleased to learn that there are only three requirements for deploying a simple contract in Solidity:

1. A text editor such as TextEdit on macOS, Gedit on Ubuntu, or Notepad on Windows. Be sure to switch to plain-text mode, which strips away all fonts, underlining, bold, hyperlinks, and italics. (Never use rich text to write code!)

2. The Mist wallet, covered in Chapter 2.

3. The Browser Solidity Compiler located at `https://ethereum.github.io/browser-solidity/` or available at the following shortlink:

   `http://compiler.eth.guide`

As we'll demonstrate in Chapter 5, all that you need to do to "upload" a contract is to copy-paste your Solidity code from your text editing application into the Solidity Browser

Compiler. From there, you'll compile the code into bytecode, and copy-paste that bytecode into Mist. It's really very easy, but let's not get bogged down in the logistics just yet. Instead, we'll examine the behavior of the sample smart contract below, so you can begin to grasp the potential of an automated contract which sends and receives money. The following example was originally written by Cyrus Adkisson (fivedogit on GitHub), a Kentuckian software engineer and Ethereum enthusiast now living in New York. It has been adapted for this book.

You'll name this contract PiggyBank, using CapsCase (rather than camelCase) per the Solidity naming conventions. You can find those naming conventions, and the rest of the Solidity style guide, at http://solidity.readthedocs.io/en/develop/style-guide.html.

Now, let's look at PiggyBank.sol:

```
contract PiggyBank {

    address creator;
    uint deposits;

// Declaring this function as public makes it accessible to other users and
smart contracts.
    function PiggyBank() public
    {
        creator = msg.sender;
        deposits = 0;
    }

// Check whether any ether has been deposited. When it is deposited, the
number of deposits go up and the total count is returned

    function deposit() payable returns (uint)
    {
        if(msg.value > 0)
            deposits = deposits + 1;
        return getNumberOfDeposits();
    }
    function getNumberOfDeposits() constant returns (uint)
    {
        return deposits;
    }

// When the external account that instantiated this contract calls it again,
it terminates and sends back its balance.
    function kill()
    {
        if (msg.sender == creator)
            selfdestruct(creator);
    }
}
```

You can find more examples of Solidity scripts for programmers of all skill levels and abilities at http://solidity.eth.guide.

Formatting Solidity Files

One major detail is missing from the preceding contract example. Every Solidity file should have (but does not require) a *version pragma*, a statement indicating which Solidity version this contract was written in. Over time, this should prevent older contracts from being rejected by future versions of the compiler.

The version pragma for this file is 0.4.7, so you should add the following to the file header:

```
pragma solidity ^0.4.7;
```

For more information on the structure of Solidity files, see http://solidity.readthedocs.io/en/develop/layout-of-source-files.html.

Tips for Reading Code

Here are seven facts that will make this contract more legible for beginners:

Computers read code from top to bottom, left to right, just like English speakers. Putting one line before another generally means the computer will see that instruction first.

Typically, programs take an input and return some kind of output. *Computable* functions (mathematical functions that can be performed by a computer) are defined as functions that can be written as algorithms.

Algorithms take in data, perform an operation on it, and return some kind of output. *Programs* are algorithms with other algorithms nested in them.

An algorithm is like a machine: you can reuse it many times. Thus, writing algorithmic instructions—*programming*—will strike you as being a lot like writing Mad Libs, which the computer will later autocomplete with information that a user (or in Ethereum, a contract) gives it, via a transaction or message call. Sometimes this information is just a number (for example, 5 ether).

Operators are the symbols between the English words, such as the equal sign, plus sign, and minus sign. These work mostly as you'd expect, with a few exceptions. You'll see Solidity operators in Table 4-1.

Types are the nouns of computer programming. So when you see a type, you know what is allowed in that space of the Mad Lib. A common type in Solidity is an address.

The original use of computers was to do math quickly. For decades, the people who used computers were mostly physicists who wanted to crunch hard math problems in order to figure out answers to questions such as this: What time and day is the best to launch Apollo 11, so that it has the shortest distance to travel to the Moon?

The EVM is much closer to this original kind of computer, but it's suited to thinking about sophisticated accounting and fiscal reconciliation, as you might learn to do in business school by programming spreadsheets in Microsoft Excel. Recall that databases are merely spreadsheets themselves, and computer programs manipulate these databases. Thus, when you *declare* something, you are telling the computer to put it in the spreadsheet—specifically, to put it in the *stack*.

The computer will figure out, on its own, how much memory to have ready to store the values in any *temporary*, or so-called *dynamic*, computations—small, pivotal logical statements used to compute contingencies such as if-then. (It's important to define the stack and heap in order to see that this is where the danger of memory-hog programs lies: in asking the computer to use more dynamic memory than it has to spare.)

Statements and Expressions in Solidity

As you'll see, there are functions all over the place in Solidity. However, they're used in different ways.

Some functions produce a *value*, such as a number, or an answer to a true/false question. What exactly this value can be is determined by Solidity's *types*, mentioned earlier; the true/false value is called a *Boolean*.

What Is an Expression?

Functions that produce a value are known as *expression functions*. Because expressions evaluate to a value of one type or another, in programming they can be used in place of values.

Other functions are *declarative*, and lead to the creation of a dedicated space in the computer's memory, which will be used each time it runs this routine. These declarative functions are important because they are crucial to writing statements.

What Is a Statement?

Speaking in grossly general terms, a *statement* tells the computer to perform an action. The computer uses expressions to figure out how to take this action, and when. Thus, computer programs are composed of statements, and statements are often composed of expressions (or other statements).

Functions, Public and Private

In JavaScript and Solidity, you can use semicolons to chain statements, and tell the computer that another statement is coming up in the code:

```
function first(); function second()
```

In Solidity, you can also declare whether you want certain functions to be available outside that program. These designations are as follows:

- `public`: Visible externally and internally (an accessor function for storage/state variables is created)

- `private`: Visible only in the current contract (default)

▓ **Note** Functions written in Solidity code are not public by default. You must declare them as public when you make them, or they will not be available to contracts outside of the one they're in.

Although this is just an introduction to code literacy, it should be enough for you to begin to decode what some of the smart contracts we'll discuss later are doing.

Value Types

When writing Solidity code, you can tell the computer what type of value to expect in each algorithmic instruction. This section describes the types of values the EVM can interpret.

Booleans

Known in code as `bool`, the Booleans are true/false expressions that evaluate to `true` or `false`.

Signed and Unsigned Integers

Known in code as `int` and `uint`, these are numbers. They can be negative if they have a sign, or minus, indicating they are signed. Unsigned integers are thus positive numbers.

Addresses

The address type holds a 20-byte value, which is the size of an Ethereum address (40 hex characters, or 160 bits). Address types also have member types.

Members of Addresses

These two members allow you to query the balance of an account, or to transfer ether to an account. Be careful with transfer in smart contracts. It's better to use a pattern where the recipient is allowed to withdraw the money, than to have a contract initiating transfers.

- `balance`
- `transfer`

Address-Related Keywords

Keywords come with the Solidity language. They are methods, so to speak, for using the language in predetermined ways. You can use these keywords in your code to accomplish common tasks needed in smart contracts. These include the following:

- `<address>.balance (uint256)`: Returns the balance of the address in wei

- `<address>.send(uint256 amount)` returns `(bool)`: Sends given amount of wei to address, and returns `false` on failure

- `this`(current contract's type): Explicitly converts to the address

- `selfdestruct(address recipient)`: Destroys the current contract, sending its funds to the given address

---

■ **Note**   It is possible to query the balance of the current contract by using the keyword `this.balance`.

Less-Common Value Types

Several other value types may be useful if you're already an advanced or intermediate programmer:

- `Dynamically sized byte arrays`
- `Fixed-point numbers`
- `Rational and integer literals`
- `String literals`
- `Hexadecimal literals`
- `Enums`

Complex (Reference) Types

Generally speaking, types in Solidity are allotted 256 bits of memory in the EVM's storage; that's 2,048 characters. Types that are any longer than that can incur more-significant gas costs to move around. You'll need to choose carefully when assigning persistent storage in the EVM's stack. Here are the complex types that exceed 256 bits:

- `Arrays`
- `Array literals / inline arrays`

- Structs

- Mappings

Arrays, structs, and other complex types have a data location that can be used by Solidity programmers to manipulate whether they are stored dynamically in memory or persistently stored. This can help you manage fees.

Global Special Variables, Units, and Functions

Global special variables can be called by any Solidity smart contract on the EVM; they're built in to the language. Most of them return information about the Ethereum chain. Units of time and ether are also globally available. Literal numbers can take a suffix of wei, finney, szabo or ether and will auto-convert between subdenominations of Ether. Ether currency numbers without a suffix are assumed to be Wei.

Time-related suffixes can be used after literal numbers to convert between units of time. Here, seconds are the base unit, and units are treated as general units. Owing to the existence of leap years, be careful when using these suffixes to calculate time, as not all years have 365 days, and not days have 24 hours.

```
1 == 1 seconds

1 minutes == 60 seconds

1 hours == 60 minutes

1 days == 24 hours

1 weeks = 7 days

1 years = 365 days
```

Block and Transaction Properties

Note that these global variables are only available in Solidity smart contracts. These shouldn't be confused with JavaScript Dapp API calls that you can make in Geth, which you'll learn about in Chapter 6.

- `block.blockhash(uint blockNumber) returns (bytes32)`:
  Hash of the given block, works for only the 256 most recent blocks

- `block.coinbase (address)`: Current block miner's address

- `block.difficulty (uint)`: Current block difficulty

- `block.gaslimit (uint)`: Current block gas limit

- `block.number (uint)`: Current block number

- `block.timestamp (uint)`: Current block timestamp

- `msg.data (bytes)`: Complete call data

- `msg.gas` (`uint`): Remaining gas

- `msg.sender` (`address`): Sender of the message (current call)

- `msg.sig` (`bytes4`): First 4 bytes of the call data (function identifier)

- `msg.value` (`uint`): Number of wei sent with the message

- `now` (`uint`): Current block timestamp (alias for `block.timestamp`)

- `tx.gasprice` (`uint`): Gas price of the transaction

- `tx.origin` (`address`): Sender of the transaction (full call chain)

Note that the values of all members of msg (that is, `msg.sender` and `msg.value`) can change for each external function call, even if they are library functions. If you desire implementation of library functions with access restrictions on the use of `msg.sender`, then you'll need to manually supply the value of `msg.sender` as an argument.

Operators Cheat Sheet

Table 4-1 shows the operators you can use in Solidity expressions.

Table 4-1.

Precedence	Description	Operator
1	Postfix increment and decrement	`++, --`
	Function-like call	`<func>(<args...>)`
	Array subscripting	`<array>[<index>]`
	Member access	`<object>.<member>`
	Parentheses	`(<statement>)`
2	Prefix increment and decrement	`++, --`
	Unary plus and minus	`+, -`
	Unary operations	`delete`
	Logical NOT	`!`
	Bitwise NOT	`~`
3	Exponentiation	`**`
4	Multiplication, division, and modulo	`*, /, %`
5	Addition and subtraction	`+, -`
6	Bitwise shift operators	`<<, >>`
7	Bitwise AND	`&`

(continued)

Table 4-1. (*continued*)

Precedence	Description	Operator
8	Bitwise XOR	^
9	Bitwise OR	|
10	Inequality operators	<, >, <=, >=
11	Equality operator, does-not-equal operator	==, !=
12	Logical AND	&&
13	Logical OR	||
14	Ternary operator	<conditional> ? <if-true> : <if-false>
15	Assignment operators	=, |=, ^=, &=, <<=, >>=, +=, -=, *=, /=, %=
16	Comma operator	,

Global Functions

In general in Solidity, special functions are mainly be used to provide information about the blockchain, but some can also perform mathematical and cryptographic functions. They are as follows:

- `keccak256(...)` `returns` `(bytes32)`: Computes the Ethereum-SHA-3 (Keccak-256) hash of the (tightly packed) arguments

- `sha3(...)` `returns` `(bytes32)`: An alias to `keccak256()`

- `sha256(...)` `returns` `(bytes32)`: Computes the SHA-256 hash of the (tightly packed) arguments. "Tightly packed" means that the arguments are concatenated without padding. To see how to add padding to arguments, see the following URL: `http://solidity.readthedocs.io/en/develop/units-and-global-variables.html#mathematical-and-cryptographic-functions`.

- `ripemd160(...)` `returns` `(bytes20)`: Computes the RIPEMD-160 hash of the (tightly packed) arguments

- `ecrecover(bytes32 hash, uint8 v, bytes32 r, bytes32 s)` `returns` `(address)`: Recovers address associated with the public key from elliptic curve signature, returns 0 on error

- `addmod(uint x, uint y, uint k)` `returns` `(uint)`: Computes `(x + y) % k`, where the addition is performed with arbitrary precision and does not wrap around at 2**256

- `mulmod(uint x, uint y, uint k) returns (uint):` Computes $(x * y) \% k$, where the multiplication is performed with arbitrary precision and does not wrap around at $2**256$

- `this (current contract's type):` The current contract, explicitly convertible to its address

It's also worth mentioning contract-related variables that can be useful in writing Solidity contracts:

- `super:` The contract one level higher in the inheritance hierarchy. For more information about inheritance, see the link in the section below.

- `selfdestruct(address recipient):` Destroys the current contract, sending its funds to the given address

- `assert(bool condition):` throws if the condition is not met.

- `revert():` abort execution and revert state changes

Exceptions and Inheritance

Some situations automatically cause exceptions. To see them all, go to `http://exceptions.eth.guide`. The Solidity language also supports multiple inheritance. Even if a contract inherits from multiple other contracts, only a single contract is created on the blockchain, the code from the base contracts is always copied into the final contract. Details about the general inheritance system can be found at `http://solidity.readthedocs.io/en/develop/contracts.html#inheritance`.

Summary

In this chapter, you took the first steps toward understanding the impact of programs written for the EVM. You also took a critical look at the way these programs can achieve a meaningful degree of Turing completeness without sacrificing the security of the network.

We've only touched briefly on the formal mathematics that make these programs so exciting for enterprise information technology. But with any luck, you've seen enough to motivate you to dig deeper into the Ethereum White Paper and Yellow Paper and see for yourself how the EVM reaches provable consensus.

In Chapter 5, you'll deploy your first token contract on the EVM. You'll also learn the social and cultural history of monetary instruments, and what it means for your understanding of the potential of Ethereum.

CHAPTER 5

■ ■ ■

Smart Contracts and Tokens

Small reusable code templates (in programming terms, classes) written in Solidity are called *smart contracts*, a nod to financial contracts. You can think of smart contracts as being suited to creating financial derivatives as a web service—with a few twists

In the preceding chapter, you learned how to use Solidity to create instructions for the Ethereum Virtual Machine. However, you stopped short of uploading your program to the EVM, a process known generally in computer application development as *deployment*. This chapter presents the process by which you can deploy your Solidity scripts to the EVM, making them available as a real product or service.

EVM as Back End

Software apps, as they currently exist for the Web, iOS, macOS, Windows, Android, Linux, and so forth, are typically discussed in two halves: the front end and the back end. The *back end* usually refers to the database and the logic around interacting with it, which (as you learned in Chapter 3) is where the program stores its information. The *front end* usually refers to the part of the application the user sees: the interface with its various labels and controls. In software interface design, *controls* is the general term for the little buttons, sliders, dials, hearts, stars, thumbs-up icons, and any other little thing you can click to make something happen.

As we've discussed already, modern-day web-enabled applications use a constellation of computers and servers, most of them running some version of Linux, which plays a vital role in a sometimes-fragile choreography of computers working together to deliver a "seamless" experience to your smartphone or computer (usually in the hopes that you'll pay for this experience).

Neither EVM nor the Bitcoin virtual machine are powerful today. The EVM will continue to get faster as the core developers iterate toward a faster block time; how that works will become clearer in Chapter 6. The takeaway for now is that the EVM is something like a replacement for the traditional application back end of a conventionally-hosted web or mobile application. Although the EVM itself is a fully fledged computer, it is not yet a complete end-to-end platform capable of hosting HTML/CSS interfaces; the most useful role it can play is as the back end to a distributed application.

© Chris Dannen 2017
C. Dannen, *Introducing Ethereum and Solidity*, DOI 10.1007/978-1-4842-2535-6_5

Smart Contracts to Dapps

A smart contract is just a unit of functionality you upload to the EVM. The term *distributed application*, or *dapp*, typically describes a web- or smartphone-accessible front end which GUI application that uses the EVM as its back end. Unless it's a very simple dapp, its back end functionality will rely on several smart contracts.

Assets Backed by Anything

In financial parlance, an *asset* is a valuable resource that you expect will produce a benefit or value in the future. Assets can include physical natural resources or abstract financial instruments, but by definition, the price of an asset should go up over time. (If it goes down, it is known as a *depreciating* asset.)

It can be said that cryptocurrencies are assets backed by anything. What exactly this means will become clear by the end of this chapter. Let's look at an example next.

Bartering with Fiat Currency

Let's say you are Alice, and you live in Japan. For the purposes of this example, assume you are paid in Japanese yen and that the prices of things such as rent, food, and basic services are denominated in yen.

Now let's say you want to pay someone in New York to do some translation work. His name is Bob. Bob the translator uses US dollars; he holds them as savings; he pays taxes in USD, too.

This creates a problem. For most people, foreign currency is not much use, and exchanging it incurs high fees and risks of price *slippage*. Slippage refers to the price dropping before you have a chance to sell your lot. Bob doesn't want yen, and Alice doesn't hold any dollars.

Although this example uses fiat moneys, Alice and Bob may as well have cabbage and glass beads to barter. Although it's true that one of them can simply drive to the nearest bureau of exchange, probably at an international airport, that's not a parsimonious solution.

With cryptocurrency, they need only establish a *conversion rate*, or multiplier, between their local currency and the cryptocurrency, and then convert the local price of the barter goods by using that multiplier. Whether they're using paper money or glass beads isn't relevant. For a trade to take place, they merely need to agree on a price.

Ether as Glass Beads

This example demonstrates one of the fundamental properties of ether and bitcoins: they are standard accounting units of value, and simultaneously media of exchange themselves. Money also serves these functions, but in actuality, the medium of exchange (paper) is just a representation of value that exists in some bank's ledger. Here, they are one in the same.

As you'll learn more in Chapter 6, these *standard account units* essentially tabulate themselves and balance the entire ledger anytime a payment moves from one place to another. This is another advantage over the money of today, which being inert has no "awareness" of other money in the system. As you may be imagining already, this makes smart contracts perfect for writing self-executing financial agreements.

A *derivative contract* is a financial "bet" between two or more parties made on the value of the underlying asset. A derivative basically says that under certain conditions, Alice agrees to pay Bob a particular amount. The number of financial derivatives currently on Earth tops $1 quadrillion dollars. They are popular little instruments!

What gives cryptocurrency the power to be used this way? The answer to that will become increasingly clear in Chapters 6 and 7, but for the sake of expediency, let's do some thought experiments that will shorten the learning curve.

Cryptocurrency Is a Measure of Time

Because cryptoassets and cryptocurrencies are impossible to counterfeit, this gives them an interesting property as a measure of time. Chapter 7 covers the issuance scheme of ether, but the point here is that these tokens are almost like the rings of a tree—their manufacture happens by a sophisticated process that cannot be "sped up." Thus when trading with someone from a faraway economy, it becomes easy to trust prices denominated in cryptocurrency, because counterfeiting isn't possible, no matter how rich or powerful the group you're trading with.

Cryptocurrencies, as of this writing, are not redeemable by any central authority for gold or fiat currency. However, they are classified as property or currency in a handful countries.[1]

Nevertheless, it can be said that cryptocurrency get their price from the marketplace: they are worth whatever someone in the marketplace will pay. This is in contrast to say, a gold-backed currency, which is redeemable from the local treasury, or even a treasury bond, and which a government guarantees it will redeem for its own fiat currency decades into the future.

As a result of its status as a decentralized digital medium of exchange, cryptocurrencies can be conceptualized as "assets backed by anything." It doesn't matter whether you're trading cattle, bananas, soybean futures, or private equities—the deal can be done in cryptocurrency. The only challenge is agreeing on a price.

Today, even if the buyer and seller agree to complete their transaction in cryptocurrency, it's likely they will quickly sell the cryptocurrency for local fiat money, to avoid price slippage. This will be less and less common as the prices of cryptocurrencies stabilize. Prices become more stable as the volume of transactions increases around the world, and the markets for trading cryptocurrencies become *deeper,* or more liquid.

Ether is similar to other cryptocurrencies such as bitcoins in this regard, but it does gain some intrinsic value from its usefulness in paying gas costs on the EVM. As we discussed in Chapter 3, this makes ether more like a *commodity* such as oil or corn, which get their respective intrinsic values from their uses as fuel and food, respectively.

---

[1]Wikipedia, "Legality of Bitcoin by Country," https://en.wikipedia.org/wiki/Legality_of_bitcoin_by_country, 2017.

Asset Ownership and Civilization

It almost goes without saying that the invention of money as a social construct is foundational to civilization. In the pantheon of Great Human Ideas, it probably ranks among innovations such as animal domestication, geometry, and stone tools.

Being highly susceptible to *the network effect,* money seems to evolve more slowly than other technologies. Because people prefer money that can be saved for long periods of time, retaining value far into the future, human societies aren't exactly eager to jump to new media of exchange, lest their savings become worthless!

The concept of network effect describes how technologies become more useful on an individual basis as their popularity grows and widens across geographical space. Being able to use bitcoins to buy retail goods all over the world is an example of its positive network effect. It makes trade possible, everywhere you go, as demonstrated in the beach vendor example in Chapter 4.

Savings, or *surplus value*, enables people to invest in the future. Whether 50,000 years ago or today, having extra food, fuel, or human labor at your disposal allows you to plan ahead and take actions that use that surplus to facilitate even bigger surpluses for future generations. An example is a community that, after a bumper crop of food, expands its population and collectively builds a dam to irrigate its fields, improving farming yields even further.

So what does this ancient history have to do with cryptocurrency?

Your Pile of Savings = Reputation

People who accumulate savings in a certain form of money, whether gold, wampum, or US dollars, will reinvest for their future. Typically, people invest in the geographic areas where they and their families reside. This is known in economics as *home bias*. It is one way that humans achieve status in a community: by donating public works, leading constructive social movements, or providing large-scale employment.

As discussed in Chapter 1, and in the preceding section, bitcoins and ether are not guaranteed by any organization to be redeemable for anything at any point in the future. Thus, a family seeking to protect its inheritance might consider bitcoins or ether a poor choice for long-term savings. The same goes for other farsighted institutions such as charities, pension funds, trusts, and endowments.

Who knows if anyone will be using these networks in 50 years! By contrast, nation-states tend to stick around for centuries. When they issue fiat currency, they also raise armies to protect their economic systems; there is no such central power enforcing the use of bitcoins or ether. To make matters even less certain, computer networks in general haven't been around long enough to really know the lifespan of their utility, as compared to, say, governments, which have existed (in some form or another) for millennia and can last thousands of years. How will cryptocurrency become more durable than the moneys we already have?

Money, Tokens, Reputation … So What?

Longevity is an asset's killer feature: the longer an asset will grow in value, and the more impossible to counterfeit it, the more desirable it is. That's why so many people store their wealth long-term in bonds and real estate.

The point of ramming home this reality is to think of bitcoins and ether as *digital collectibles*. As you'll see, this is the most useful approach when considering the many uses of smart contracts. After all, learning how to write programs for the EVM is just as challenging as figuring out what to build. And the long history of money gives us many clues as to what kind of novel business transactions or social constructs may be possible with this new asset class.

Much has been written about the potential of Ethereum to bring to bear the real potential of the Internet, especially the Internet of Things.[2] From the literature about Ethereum that's already on the Web, it's easy to imagine industrial or retail scenarios in which small computers can execute microtransactions.

But this view limits us to transactions we already make today. The promise of the Ethereum and Bitcoin protocols is the introduction of new kinds of transactions and instruments. In this Internet of Things, what about the world of everyday consumer goods? Aren't they "things" too? Let's say you print an Ethereum address (a public key) on a physical item, and it belongs to a smart contract.

Or more practically, consider a QR code, shown in Figure 5-1, which is a machine-readable code in a nested-square pattern. This one points to the links for this book, http://eth.guide. If you go to the iOS App Store or Google Play apps on your mobile devices, you should find any number of free QR code reader apps. Just search *QR reader*. You can imagine how these QR codes, printed on everyday valuables such as clothing, jewelry, artworks, or other physical goods, could combine the concepts of derivative contracts, everyday reloadable debit cards, and collectibles.

Figure 5-1. *QR codes provide an easy way for machines to read cryptocurrency addresses and URLs. This one goes to* http://eth.guide.

Coins are Collectibles

Before going any further down this rabbit hole, let's encounter some anthropological history courtesy of Nick Szabo, a cryptocurrency pioneer whose prolific web essays influenced many of today's cryptocurrency enthusiasts and cypherpunks.

---

[2]ConsenSys Media, "Programmable Blockchains in Context: Ethereum's Future," https://medium.com/consensys-media/programmable-blockchains-in-context-ethereum-s-future-cd8451eb421e#.rwdqmpvu0, 2015.

In 2002, Szabo wrote about the intersection of physical goods representing abstract value throughout the course of human history. These collectibles allowed us to engage in bigger, more complex financial transactions, he explained. [3]

Collectibles were crucial in making these kinds of transactions possible for the first time. Collectibles augmented our large brains and language as solutions to the Prisoner's Dilemma that keeps almost all animals from cooperating via delayed reciprocation with nonkin.

Without a trustworthy collectible to trade back and forth, you might not be willing to trade resources with anyone outside your extended familial network. This doesn't bode well for peaceful coexistence in larger nation-states.

The Function of Collectibles in Human Systems

Keeping track of favors over time is a major function of money: to serve as a closed accounting system for a community to keep track of favors owed and favors given. This gets useful as bigger and bigger groups try to interact and cooperate.

Using collectibles to count favors is the essence of primordial accounting. Eventually, the value of these favors became abstracted, leading to the generalized instruments of value such as gold. This accounts for the modern-day association between wealth and esteem.

Ethereum and Bitcoin strike at the heart of a problem that is tens of thousands of years old, which is that reputation-accounting a natural human behavior, but also an imperfect one. Szabo continues:

Reputational beliefs can suffer from two major kinds of errors—errors of about which person did what, and errors in appraising the value or damages caused by that act. In both Homo sapiens neanderthalis and Homo sapiens, with the same large brain size, it is quite likely that every local clan member kept track of every other local clan member's favors.... Between clans within a tribe both favor tracking and collectibles were used.

Two clans within a tribe exchanging collectibles within a closed system is something like a private bank database. Or a private blockchain. Szabo writes:

Between tribes, collectibles entirely replaced reputation as the enforcer of reciprocation, although violence still played a major role in enforcing rights as well as being a high transaction cost that prevented most kinds of trade.

---

[3]Nick Szabo, "Shelling Out: The Origins of Money," http://nakamotoinstitute.org/shell-ing-out/, 2002.

Just like the banks of today, human groups of yesteryear had trouble trading outside their accounting system. Whose money system do you use? Who keeps track of inter-tribe favors? No wonder there was so much bloodshed: the opportunity for cheating is just too persistent.

Early Counterfeiting

The solution to inter-tribe trade was to use rare art objects: not just rare earth elements, but any objects that were not trivial to find or create from scratch. They couldn't be just any set of beautiful objects. They had to be hard to come by, or the product of skilled craftsmanship, which ensured that each collectible represented a certain amount of human work-time. The resulting collectible can be considered "proof of work" by the craftsman. And thus we're back to the concept from earlier: bitcoins and ether as a store of time. As Szabo says:

> *It had to have certain functional properties, such as the security of being wearable on the person, compactness for hiding or burial, and unforgeable costliness. That costliness must have been verifiable by the recipient of the transfer—using many of the same skills that collectors use to appraise collectibles today.*

Jewelry and Art as Money

There's perhaps nothing more essential to human economic progress as a reliable set of collectibles that can be used as money. This is because money facilitates cooperation. Szabo goes so far as to say that cooperation is our defining adaptive feature at the group level:

> *Today, most large animals on the planet are afraid of projectiles—an adaption to only one species of predator.*

Yes, that's us, the tool-creating apes who hunt like wolves and live in social colonies like termites! In a sense, modern cryptocurrencies are a super-lubricant for our sophisticated human cooperative systems, because they introduce the building blocks of an immutable system of account that can span the geography of the entire world.

The Step Toward Banknotes

Money, reputation, and status have always been wrapped up together. It makes sense that primitive valuables were *things you could wear*; think gold jewelry or diamond-studded crowns. After all, why not show off the status that your hard work (or luck!) had bestowed on you?

However, as a society gets wealthier, everyone gets to own a little gold; then a little more, then a little more. A rising tide creates markets for new goods and services that allow the wealthiest people to enjoy themselves in ways that also exhibit their social status.

At some point, it's too much to wear and carry, and people begin competing on abstractions such as brand name of goods, or the particular school where their children go.

By this point in a developing society, there's enough wealth stocked up in the banks that individual account holders begin trading in *banknotes*. How this works is best explained by economic researcher Martin Armstrong.[4] He says:

> *The distinction between banknotes and deposit receipts issued by goldsmiths was a simple one. A receipt for deposit was transformed into a banknote if the receipt was payable to the "bearer" rather than an account. Therefore, Paterson's Bank of England cleverly created the circulating notes by de facto since its receipts were payable to the "bearer," thereby creating circulating "banknotes" when there was no provision for such an instrument.*

Bitcoin revised this relationship only slightly by creating bearer accounts; whoever has the password and private key of an account is by default the owner. Bitcoin addresses, like Ethereum addresses, are not registered to individuals. They are created pseudonymously.

Ether is like an issuance of banknotes that is also redeemable for computing time on the EVM.

Platforms for High-Value Digital Collectibles

In a digital context, a reliable store of time has incredible potential as a platform for digital collectibles: valuable items that can be displayed, worn, or hung in one's personal space—either online or in real life—and that are not possible to knock off, nor easily stolen from their rightful owner.

When most people think of the Internet of Things, they think of sensor motes, self-diagnosing industrial equipment, and driverless vehicles. The Internet of Value, a euphemism referring to blockchain technologies, one of the many metaphors used to represent Ethereum and Bitcoin conceptually. But rather than think abstractly, it may be more useful to think about the potential in terms of valuable artwork, jewelry, fashion, or premium goods that look much like today's, but feature verifiable provenance and ownership stored on a blockchain.

In the future, the ownership, value, and provenance of a physical thing may never be "forgotten" as long as the blockchain where it was inventoried is still up and running. There will be no *Antiques Roadshow* on TV in 100 years. (We could even write a smart contract to take that bet!)

---

[4]Armstrong Economics, "Money and the Evolution of Banking," www.armstrongeconomics.com/research/monetary-history-of-the-world/historical-outline-origins-of-money/money-and-the-evolution-of-banking/, 2016.

Tokens Are a Category of Smart Contract

Generally speaking, the Ethereum protocol prides itself on being *featureless*, which is one reason that tokens (as a concept) overlap so heavily with smart contracts (as a concept). Tokens are just one application of smart contract functionality on the EVM.

■ **Note**   In this chapter, you will deploy your own token. Tokens are one specific (and popular) application of smart contracts. Thus, the Mist wallet makes it especially easy to make tokens. There is currently no other category of smart contract which is accommodated this way in Mist.

That said, Ethereum does make provisions for one common use-case of smart contracts, which is a *subcurrency*, a.k.a. token. In the hopes of making it easy to get up and running, the Ethereum developers have put an easy-to-use template inside the Mist wallet for quickly launching your own tokens. Presumably, other templates for common smart contracts will follow. But at present, the one we get out of the box is the ability to create a custom unit of value which can be passed around, alongside ether, within the EVM.

If you were to phrase the user-friendly token-making progress as an elevator pitch for its value proposition to users, it would be something like this: "ultra-secure digital monetary system with automatic ledger balancing delivered as a service."

Now that you've gotten a taste of the historic potential of Ethereum and Bitcoin to create a new era of cryptocollectibles and smart devices, let's get back to the brass tacks of deploying a token in the wild.

■ **Note**   This chapter contains exercises that use the Mist wallet you installed in Chapter 2. After installation on your machine, it may appear labeled as Ethereum Wallet. This book refers to it as Mist to differentiate it from the many other Ethereum wallets available for desktop and mobile computers today.

Tokens as Social Contracts

Tokens are sometimes called *coins*, as you learned in the Chapter 3. You also learned that tokens themselves are smart contracts. (With enough repetition, these terms will hopefully enter your natural vocabulary by the end of this book!)

But tokens themselves (like all forms of money) can also be seen as social contracts, or agreements between groups of users. In plain English, the implicit agreement of a group using a token would be as follows: "We all agree this token is money in our community." It's also a tacit agreement not to counterfeit, undermining the system!

The closest thing we have to a social contract in software form today is probably the end-user license agreements, or EULAs, that users sign when they create an account on services such as Facebook, Twitter, iTunes, or Gmail. This agreement usually includes language barring activities such as spamming other users, which would degrade the user experience.

Thinking this way allows us to imagine how our digital media and digital goods today might become *digital collectibles* that are discussed, marketed, sold, and displayed inside the social networks of the future, in which online artifacts like selfies and podcasts can be sold, licensed, or rented for fees of arbitrary size.

Tokens Are a Great First App

When making a token, consider that it is only as valuable as the community using it believes it will be. Thus, it is far easier to launch a token into an existing community that already trades using some kind of money or scrip.

However, making sub currencies is not the only use of a *cryptoasset*. The concept of an asset is highly generalized. Assets, in the form of financial contracts or smart contracts, can be used to represent shares of equity, or lottery tickets, or just scrip within a local economy. The price can be determined by the market, or it can be pegged to another asset. The rules are largely up to you.

■ **Note** *Scrip* is a term derived from the word *subscription*. It has a variety of definitions going back in history, but refers primarily to an IOU. It can also refer to private currency such as air miles or rewards points. It's used in this book to mean a general unit of account: the "beans" used by the EVM's giant decentralized bean counter!

In Ethereum, tokens exist within, and rely upon, the public blockchain: you can create a *subcurrency* of ether, but ether will always remain the priviliged token with which miners and gas costs are paid. If you want a purely independent blockchain network, you can create your own private blockchain and be completely disconnected from the main Ethereum chain.

Making a subcurrency is easier and will satisfy most use cases for curious developers. If you're working at an institution interested in using its own blockchain, never fear: you will look at making your own private chain and cryptoeconomy that is separate and distinct from the Ethereum public chain in Chapter 8.

Creating a Token on the Testnet

You'll need to connect to the Ropsten testnet and get used to sending ether around before you can deploy a contract.

■ **Note**   The Ropsten testnet was formerly called Morden, so you may still see that name in older documentation.

Launch the Mist wallet on your desktop computer. Navigate to the Develop menu of the Mist wallet, and you should find a Network menu that allows you to select the testnet, as shown in Figure 5-2.

Figure 5-2. *Connecting to the testnet*

Once you're using the testnet, you should see an alert in the Mist browser highlighted in red, as shown in Figure 5-3.

Figure 5-3. *Once connected to the testnet, you'll see an indicator in the Mist UI*

Getting Test Ether from the Faucet

In Ethereum, it is trivial to set up a *faucet* that spouts faux ether you can use on the Ropsten testnet. In this section, you won't set up your own faucet, but will use a third-party faucet pictured in Figure 5-4 and available at http://faucet.ropsten.be:3001/.

You'll also find an up-to-date shortlink to this faucet at http://faucet.eth.guide. Follow these steps to receive testnet ether from the faucet:

1. After making sure your Mist wallet is on the testnet with the steps above, create an address if you haven't already. Copy this long hexidecial address (beignning with 0x...) to your system clipboard and then paste it into the address field:

2. To get ether, click the button entitled "send me 1 test ether."

99

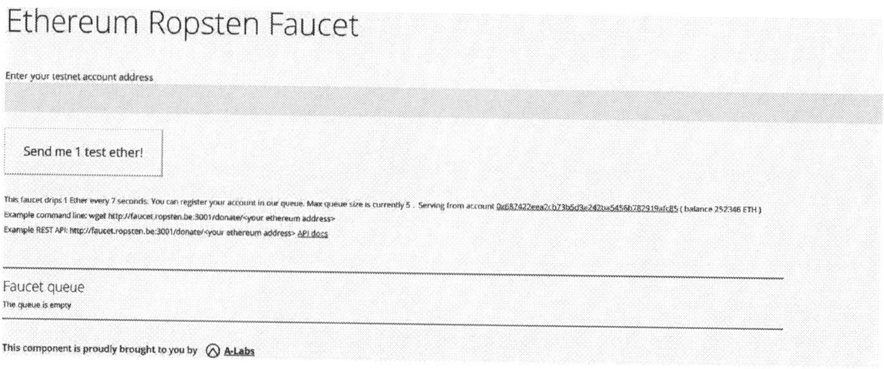

Ethereum Ropsten Faucet

Enter your testnet account address

_____

| Send me 1 test ether! |

This faucet drips 1 Ether every 7 seconds. You can register your account in our queue. Max queue size is currently 5 . Serving from account 0x687422eea2cb73b6d3e242ba5456b782919afc85 (balance 252346 ETH)
Example command line: wget http://faucet.ropsten.be:3001/donate/<your ethereum address>
Example REST API: http://faucet.ropsten.be:3001/donate/<your ethereum address> API docs

Faucet queue
The queue is empty

This component is proudly brought to you by ⋀ A-Labs

Figure 5-4. *The Ethereum testnet comes with the facility for dispensing test ether that can be used while writing or debugging contracts*

If you'd like to test out the transfer of ether, you can do that by transferring test ether from one address in your Mist wallet to another address in your Mist wallet. To do this: Go back to Mist and create a new wallet address in the Home view. You can use the Send dialog box to send ether from one of your wallet addresses to another. It will be approximately the same speed whether you are sending ether to yourself or to someone on the other side of the world; that's the beauty of distributed systems.

The testnet also has a blockchain explorer, where you can see all your testnet transactions. Simply enter one your testnet Mist addresses into the search box at the following testnet blockchain explorer, and you'll see all its transactions listed:
https://testnet.etherscan.io/

Now that we've messed around with test ether on the Ropsten chain, let's take the next step toward making your own ether subcurrency, also known as a token, with zero coding.

_____

■ **Note**   What separates the testnet and the main network? They are different chains. Kind of like a computer with many hard drives, your Ethereum node can connect to many chains.

_____

In the next section, you will copy and paste your way to the future of money-as-a-web-service. In other words, you'll use boilerplate code to create your own custom accounting and value transfer system—your own asset database, secured by the public Ethereum chain!

EXERCISE: CREATE A CUSTOM TOKEN WITH NO CODE

Creating your own token can be done in about 5 minutes. All you need is the Mist browser, which you downloaded in Chapter 2, and a text editor. If you're using macOS, Windows, or Ubuntu, your computer comes with a text editor application, but you can also opt for a third-party app such as Sublime Text.

Recall that download links for all Ethereum client applications, including Mist, can be found at http://clients.eth.guide.

■ **Note** In this exercise, you will create your token on the testnet for the time being. Recall that all smart contracts, including tokens, cost money (ether) to deploy on the EVM. It's not particularly dangerous to create a token on the main network, but you will need to pay a small amount of real ether to deploy it there, and there's no sense in wasting real money—no matter how small the amount!

If you've programmed before, you'll know that most developer environments force you to work in an integrated suite of applications to create your application. In the Ethereum protocol, it's possible to write and deploy an application by using just your computer's text editor and the Mist wallet. Pretty amazing!

In preparation, open the Ethereum Mist wallet. Click the Contracts tab at the upper right, as shown in Figure 5-5.

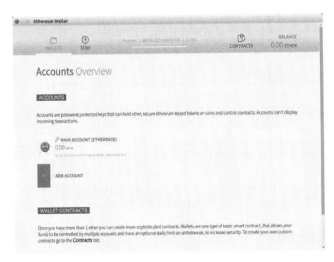

Figure 5-5. *The Contracts tab is where you can paste and deploy your contract*

1. Click the Deploy New Contract option, as shown in Figure 5-6.

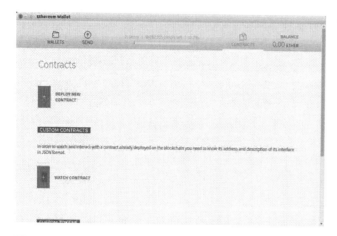

Figure 5-6. *Click the Deploy New Contract option to enter contract code*

2. Navigate to this book's GitHub project (https://github.com/
   chrisdannen/Introducing-Ethereum-and-Solidity/) and
   find the document mytoken.sol. Copy the code from this file. It
   looks like the code in Figure 5-7.

Figure 5-7. *The code for this sample project, viewed in GitHub*

3. Copy this code. Then go back to the Mist wallet and paste the code in the Deploy view, in the box labeled Solidity Contract Source Code, shown in Figure 5-8. Be sure to replace everything when you paste; the content shown here is placeholder text.

```
SOLIDITY CONTRACT SOURCE          CONTRACT BYTE CODE
        CODE

1    pragma solidity ^0.4.2;
2
3 ▾  contract MyContract {
4         /* Constructor */
5 ▾       function MyContract() {
6
7
8
9         }
10  }
```

Figure 5-8. *Replace all the placeholder text when you paste in your contract source code*

4. Now the code should look like the view in Figure 5-9.

```
        SOLIDITY CONTRACT SOURCE CODE                        CONTRACT BYTE CODE

1    pragma solidity ^0.4.8;
2 ▾  contract MyToken {
3         /* Public variables of the token */
4         string public name;
5         string public symbol;
6         uint8 public decimals;
7
8         /* This creates an array with all balances */
9         mapping (address => uint256) public balanceOf;
10
11        /* This generates a public event on the blockchain that will notify clients */
12        event Transfer(address indexed from, address indexed to, uint256 value);
13
14        /* Initializes contract with initial supply tokens to the creator of the contract *
15 ▾      function MyToken(uint256 _supply, string _name, string _symbol, uint8 _decimals) {
16            /* if supply not given then generate 1 million of the smallest unit of the toke
17            if (_supply == 0) _supply = 1000000;
18
19            /* Unless you add other functions these variables will never change */
20            balanceOf[msg.sender] = _supply;
21            name = _name;
22            symbol = _symbol;
23
24            /* If you want a divisible token then add the amount of decimals the base unit
25            decimals = _decimals;
26        }
27
28        /* Send coins */
29 ▾      function transfer(address _to, uint256 _value) {
30 ◀
```

Figure 5-9. *After you've pasted in your contract code, you should see a new drop-down become available at the right of the screen*

103

5. Now you'll see the name of the contract autoload into the menu at right. It should be called *My Token.* Select it. The fields shown in Figure 5-10 should appear.

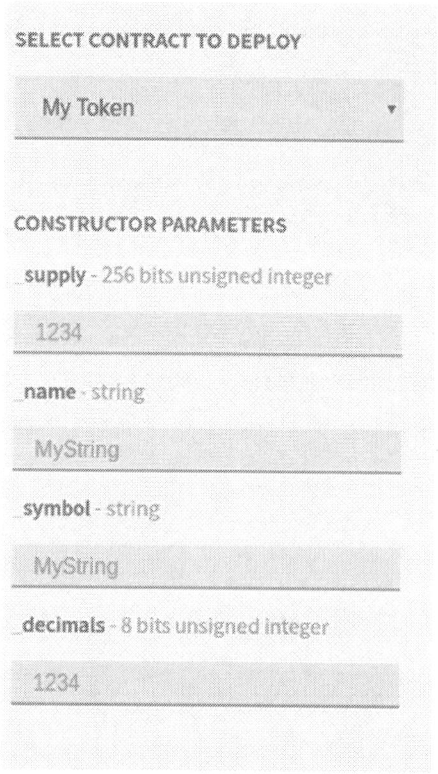

SELECT CONTRACT TO DEPLOY

My Token ▾

CONSTRUCTOR PARAMETERS

supply - 256 bits unsigned integer

1234

name - string

MyString

symbol - string

MyString

decimals - 8 bits unsigned integer

1234

Figure 5-10. After you paste in contract code, you'll need to enter your token paramters

■ **Note** Notice the light-gray text after each label, and recall our discussion of types from Chapter 4. You'll see that the supply and decimal place fields need to be of the type uint, or positive numbers; the rest can be strings of arbitrary text or numbers.

6. Next let's fill out these fields:

Supply: How many tokens do you want to create?

Name: What should this token be called?

Symbol: Use any symbol on the keyboard as your "dollar sign."

Decimals: Do you want 100 subunits to a token, as in dollars and cents? Or 1,000? Or 10,000?

7. Now that you've set parameters, scroll to the bottom and click the Deploy button. You can leave the fee slider at the default; anything your token deployment doesn't spend will get refunded.

8. In the Wallets tab, scroll down to the latest transactions and you should see the address of the contract you just deployed.

To see your balance of tokens, you'll need to "watch" this token. That's the subject of the next exercise.

After you've created a token, you can send it to anyone else with a Mist wallet, after they've given you their wallet address. In order for them to see it, you'll have to tell them to "watch" for it. More details about these particularities follow.

EXERCISE: WATCH TOKENS

Whether it's a token you created yourself, or a token created by some big organization, all tokens are created equal in the Ethereum system. Your Mist wallet will ignore them unless told to do otherwise. Much as your iPhone wouldn't download every app in the App Store, Mist lets you seek out and download the ones you want.

As you can see from the Watch Contract dialog box in Figure 5-11, you don't need much to follow a token. Let's dive in.

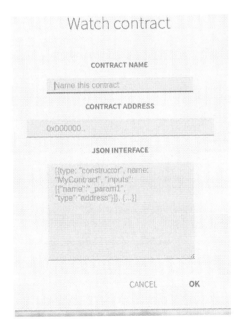

Figure 5-11. Knowing the basics about a token allows Mist to keep track of your balance in that token

105

After a smart contract has been uploaded to the EVM, that's all it takes for the world to access it. Downloading apps isn't necessary in the Mist wallet paradigm, although the code for contracts does get put into each block, and thus passively downloaded onto any machine that is mining.

Because all smart contracts are both delivered as a service and executed locally at approximately the same time, it's almost as if you have the entire App Store already on your machine, and you simply need to invoke an app.

This invocation of a specific app, or contract, is most common in the use case of the token category of apps that you're currently exploring. In token terminology, we call this *watching* a token. Because tokens are such a common and useful application of smart contracts, you will find a ready-made token-watching interface in the Mist wallet. Here's how it works:

1. Go back to the Contracts tab in Mist.

2. Click Watch Token.

3. Paste in the token address. Write in the name of this token, if it has one.

4. You don't need to enter anything in the JSON box because Mist comes with a front-end interface for tokens. You will enter some data here when you deploy a bespoke contract later in this chapter.

5. Click the Watch button. You should now see this token's balance show up in your main Mist wallet dashboard.

Watching other contracts requires searching the contract address in a blockchain explorer. Many blockchain explorers are available for the Ethereum chain, which you'll find at http://explorer.eth.guide.

In the exercises in this chapter, you will deploy contracts on the testnet, so they will not be viewable in the preceding explorers. Explorers are like database readers, and the testnet is a different database (or chain) than the main network, where real ether is transacted, and for which the vast majority of blockchain explorers provide an interface.

Registering Your Tokens

Tokens are publicly discoverable, provided you register your tokens with a blockchain explorer such as Etherscan and conform to the ERC Token Standard. ERC stands for Ethereum Request for Comment, and refers to a common convention called RFC (Request for Comment) used by the principal technical development and standards-setting bodies for the Internet.

In addition to ERC documents, Ethereum community development is also led by Ethereum Improvement Proposals, or EIPs. You can a see a list all the preprogrammed standardized functions accessible to a standard token at https://github.com/ethereum/EIPs/issues/20. The Ethereum venture studio ConsenSys has also released free and open source standard smart contract code at https://github.com/ConsenSys/Tokens. Both of these URLs are also linked at http://tokens.eth.guide.

Deploying Your First Contract

The launch of the Ethereum protocol did feature several standard contracts, but these have been largely deprecated. As of this writing, only tokens are standardized, as evidenced by the token wizard you just used in the Mist browser to deploy your tokens.

However, thanks to Gavin Wood, you have a group of simple contracts released under the Apache 2 license, with which you can experiment. Below, we'll deploy one of these contracts, but you can find the rest at https://github.com/ethcore/contracts. While no longer considered "standard," the contract below is a useful learning tool because it effectively demonstrates some of the autonomy exhibited by smart contracts, as you saw them in Chapter 4—in particular, how they can hold your ether, and give it back only if you instruct them in advance.

■ **Note**   Recall that there are two types of accounts in Ethereum: the first are smart contract accounts, and the second are externally owned accounts that are controlled by a key pair and usually held by a human or an external server.

If the lack of standard contract libraries seems strange, never fear. Plenty of third-party groups are creating standard smart contract libraries, some of them even specialized to certain industries. Many resources including Solidity sample contracts, best practices, guides, tutorials, and contract libraries are listed at http://solidity.eth.guide.

Double-check before you deploy contracts for the first time that you are indeed on the testnet! Whether you are on macOS, Windows, or Ubuntu, you will see the Develop menu in the top bar, as shown in Figure 5-12 in the Ubuntu 14.04 environment. Also note that Mist can perform mining on the testnet. This allows you to test contracts locally. More details on that in the next sections.

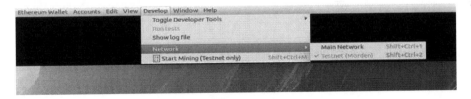

Figure 5-12. *Double-check you are on the testnet*

EXERCISE: DEPLOY A SIMPLE CONTRACT IN 5 MINUTES

The Owned contract is perhaps the most popular smart contract learning aid. That's because it establishes one of the fundamental relationships possible in the EVM: the relationship between an externally owned account and a contract account. Make no mistake: these accounts are discrete entities, but relationships between a contract account and an external account can be programmed.

Recall that a contract account, *if incorrectly programmed*, could conceivably lock up money sent to it—without offering any recourse for getting that money back. There are no backdoors into contracts, even for the people who create them. The EVM is fairly unforgiving this way! This is also why we use the testnet and fake ether, which we get from a faucet when creating contracts in this sandbox environment.

You will find the contract code at https://github.com/chrisdannen/Introducing-Ethereum-and-Solidity/.

Because of the risky nature of contracts, it's important to practice writing contracts that you, the programmer, can control. Hence the named for the Owned contract: it teaches how to write a little ether class that is controlled by other Solidity code. Let's have a look at owned.sol:

```
//! Owned contract.
//! By Gav Wood (Ethcore), 2016.
//! Released under the Apache Licence 2.

pragma solidity ^0.4.6;

contract Owned {
modifier only_owner { if (msg.sender != owner) return; _; }

event NewOwner(address indexed old, address indexed current);

function setOwner(address _new) only_owner { NewOwner(owner, _new);
owner = _new; }

address public owner = msg.sender;

}
```

■ **Note**   Don't forget to add the Solidity version pragma as the first line of your smart contract before you deploy it. This isn't strictly necessary, but it helps prevent compiler errors.

You'll deploy the Owned contract in a moment, at which point the EVM will give you back a contract address. Once it's uploaded to the testnet, you can paste this contract address into the Mist wallet in the To field and send it some amount of ether to activate it. This would make your external account msg.sender, and therefore the owner of this contract.

What does this mean? This contract will be hosted forever on the EVM and it has one function: it belongs to whichever person or contract who calls it, at that given address. Keep in mind that if someone else copies this contract and deploys it themselves, it's on the same EVM but lives at a different address. It would be a separate instance of the same contract.

Same House, Different Address

In computing, we might say that two people deploying the same exact contract on the same EVM, at necessarily different addresses, equates roughly to building two houses from the same blueprint. They can't occupy the same physical space, but are merely *instances* of the same class, or blueprint, writ in real life.

Owned.sol is the golden retriever of smart contracts: call it, and it runs right over and assigns you ownership of itself—regardless of whether you are a human operating an external account, or simply another smart contract that is calling owned.sol programmatically.

If Alice uploads owned.sol to the EVM from India, it can be accessed as a local script, and thus extended, by a contract you upload to the EVM from New York. Cool, huh?

In the last deployment—the token—you simply pasted in the Solidity code and let Mist do the work. That's cool but a little too easy. To learn more about what's happening under the hood, let's manually compile the Solidity code into EVM bytecode by using the online compiler. As a reminder, you can find the online compiler at http://compiler.eth.guide.

After you have the compiler open in your browser, return to this book's GitHub page (https://github.com/chrisdannen/Introducing-Ethereum-and-Solidity/). Let's compile and test the Owned contract. Locate the Solidity script named owned.sol in the Github repo and open it to complete the following steps:

■ **Note**   Copy all the text in the file. This includes the version pragma header at the top. This tells the compiler which version of the Solidity language this contract was written in.

---

1.   Copy the text of this contract onto your computer's clipboard. (Ctrl+C on Windows or Linux, and Command+C on Mac.)

2.   Paste your code (Ctrl+V or Command+V) into the main text box of the browser compiler. If there's some sample code there, clear it all out first. You don't want any of that junk in your nice clean contract. It should look something like Figure 5-13.

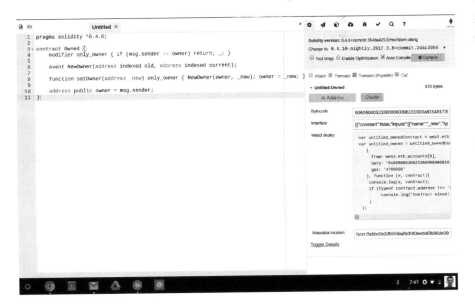

Figure 5-13.   *Paste in the contract code to the compiler window in your browser*

3. Click the Compile button, and your contract will compile. Select the bytecode that appears in the bytecode field and copy that to your clipboard.

4. Go back to the Mist browser.

5. Repeat the Contract Deploy process from the Token contract: in the Mist wallet, go to the Contracts tab in the upper right, and click Deploy New Contract. Paste your new bytecode into the Contract Bytecode box.

6. Scroll to the bottom and click the Deploy button.

7. In the Wallets tab, scroll down to the latest transactions and you should see the address of the contract you just deployed.

8. Go through the same Watch Contract flow as you did with the token. Paste the contract address you got from your transaction feed, and name the contract **Owned**. This time, you'll add some JSON code in the box.

9. Next, return to the Browser-Solidity compiler and copy the content in the JSON Interface section of the page. This provides a basic front end for your contract, based on what the compiler could glean from your Solidity code.

Playing with Contracts

Now that your contract is deployed with an interface in Mist, you can activate it. To call a contract in the EVM, you do not necessarily need to send any ether; you can call it simply by sending zero ether to the contract address. Boom, now you are the owner! If this doesn't work, be sure that the contract was uploaded to the testnet, and that the Mist you are using to send the zero-ether transaction is also on the testnet.

For the Owned contract, activation is a yes-or-no question. You can call it with zero ether or 100. In more-sophisticated contracts, the amount you send is vital to how the contract behaves subsequently after being called.

Owned is just a reference contract that might live on the EVM, a pivotal public resource contract with lots of incoming references, for years and years.

By working with a small smart contract, you can see how smart contracts are used piecemeal to cobble together entire distributed apps, largely using boilerplate code or public-use instances, enabling the end programmer to just write the most customized of functionality, reducing the room for error.

Summary

In this chapter, you were able to deploy two separate smart contracts. In the process, you learned about the most basic application you can write for the EVM, a token contract. You also considered some of the unique properties of distributed programs by playing with owned.sol. By now, you should begin to see how powerful the Ethereum protocol can be, and how simple and easy it is to deploy contracts that leverage the power of the network.

Next, it's worth learning more about how the EVM network-database achieves consensus: a process known as proof-of-work mining. That is the subject of the next chapter.

■ ■ ■

CHAPTER 6

Mining Ether

Mining is the process by which the Ethereum network reaches consensus about the order of transactions in a given period of time, which in turn allows the EVM to make valid state transitions

We learned a lot about how the EVM works in Chapter 3, but one area of its functionality—mining—requires its own chapter. Mining is important because it is the process by which consensus is reached in the system, and by which ether is created. Bitcoin also uses mining to reach consensus, but the way things work in Ethereum is a little bit different, owing to its ability to execute smart contracts.

What's the Point?

In the pursuit of something as idealistic as the EVM, a world computer that anyone can use, it's important to be realistic about how its advantages and disadvantages are assessed. At this point, you may be wondering whether such a sophisticated (or complicated) network can ever succeed.

The chapter that follows describes a system that, for some readers, will appear unapproachable and overwhelming. However, like many of our modern-day systems, it's important to understand the problem being solved. The solutions may change, and indeed the Ethereum protocol (like the Bitcoin protocol) will adapt and change over time. But the problem of trust in human societies is persistent.

It's also important to recall that the creators of decentralized networks are cryptographers at heart, interested in one goal: the creation of an accessible, trustless world computer that is much harder to destroy than it was to create. To quote Vitalik Buterin:

> *Cryptography is truly special in the 21st century because cryptography is one of the very few fields where adversarial conflict continues to heavily favor the defender. Cypherpunk philosophy is fundamentally about leveraging this precious asymmetry to create a world that better preserves the autonomy of the individual, and cryptoeconomics is to some extent*

© Chris Dannen 2017
C. Dannen, *Introducing Ethereum and Solidity*, DOI 10.1007/978-1-4842-2535-6_6

an extension of that, except this time protecting the safety and liveness of complex systems of coordination and collaboration, rather than simply the integrity and confidentiality of private messages. Systems that consider themselves ideological heirs to the cypherpunk spirit should maintain this basic property, and be much more expensive to destroy or disrupt than they are to use and maintain. The "cypherpunk spirit" isn't just about idealism; making systems that are easier to defend than they are to attack is also simply sound engineering.[1]

With that in mind, let's begin our discussion of mining with the issuance of ether itself.

Ether's Source

Ether is considered the *native token* of Ethereum because it gets created out of thin air during the mining process, as payment for mining work performed by computers. Because mining is computationally intensive, it can generate large electricity costs for your home or office. Miners take their rewards seriously.

Mining rewards are accomplished through an account balance increase programmed into the EVM's state transition function. They are payable to whichever random miner finds a block. (In order to mine, you need to pass the mining method an Ethereum address to pay, so that it knows whose balance to increase.)

Let's take a closer look by starting with some vocabulary definitions.

Defining Mining

In Ethereum, *miners* refers to a vast global network of computers, operated mostly by enthusiasts in their homes and offices, running Ethereum nodes that are paid in ether tokens for the work of executing smart contracts and validating the canonical order of transactions around the world. The process of mining is undertaken by each individual node, but the term also refers to the collective effort of the network: individual nodes mine, and the network itself can be said to be *secured* by mining.

Miners process transactions in groups known as *blocks*. We previously defined a block, in the abstract, as a collated set of transactions that take place over a given period of time. However, a block can also refer to the data object containing those transactions, stored on Ethereum nodes. Each time a node starts, it must download the blocks it missed while offline. Each block contains some metadata from the previous block, to prove it is authentic and build on the existing blockchain.

The "true" order of transactions is hard for the network to determine. Mining nodes in different parts of the world may receive new transactions out of order. In fact, there

---

[1]Vitalik Buterin, "A Proof of Stake Design Philosophy," https://medium.com/@VitalikButerin/a-proof-of-stake-design-philosophy-506585978d51#.7n3x85gvs, 2016.

exist many more incorrectly ordered blocks than correctly ordered ones. Some malicious node operators may modify their machines to submit fraudulent blocks in the hopes of sending free ether to their accounts.

Thus, *mining* can properly be defined as dedicating computational effort to the bolstering of a given version of history as the correct one. The mining process is computationally demanding for nodes because it involves executing a memory-intensive hashing algorithm known as as a *proof-of-work algorithm*. The proof-of-work algorithm (or PoW algorithm) for the Ethereum protocol is Ethash, a new function created by the core developers in order to address the problem of mining centralisation evident in Bitcoin. You'll sometimes hear this algorithm referred to as Ethereum's *consensus algorithm* or *consensus engine*. The block that is selected as canonical is the one with the greatest amount of proof of work behind it. What this means will become clear by the end of the chapter; for now, let's continue to define some key terms.

The amount of computation a miner can apply to the network is known as hashpower. *Hashpower* is a reflection of an individual computer's parts and specifications—in particular, the speed, power, and quantity of graphics processing cards; the computer system's overall power supply; and the availability of adequate voltage from the wall outlet and the breaker panel it's connected to.

The cryptographic proof which results from mining can be completed more quickly when more hashpower is applied. Therefore, miners often form *mining pools* to increase their chances of winning rewards, which they then split among the group.

Now that we've defined some vocabulary, let's talk about why mining is necessary in the first place and how exactly it works in Ethereum.

Versions of the Truth

To understand why there are so many versions of transaction history, let's turn to Gavin Wood, who says it best in the Ethereum Yellow Paper:

> *Since the system is decentralized and all parties have an opportunity to create a new block on some older preexisting block, the resultant structure is necessarily a tree of blocks. In order to form a consensus as to which path, from root (the genesis block) to leaf (the block containing the most recent transactions) through this tree structure, known as the blockchain, there must be an agreed-upon scheme.*[2]

We'll talk more about this tree structure in later sections. For now, simply note that when nodes disagree about which root-to-leaf path is the true blockchain, then a state fork happens, and that is usually disastrous—the equivalent of the EVM splitting into two EVMs. We'll talk more about forks later in this chapter, too.

---

[2]Gavin Wood, "Ethereum Yellow Paper," https://github.com/ethereum/yellowpaper, 2016.

Difficulty, Self-Regulation, and the Race for Profit

Mining is designed to be a money-maker for the people who engage in it; they are paid for providing security to the network. What exactly is drawing thousands of IT hobbyists and professionals to build and run these machines at their own expense?

The first thing to know is that time is a factor! When a new cryptocurrency launches, miners rush to turn on their machines. With less competition for fees in the early days, they earn more. Even better, tokens belonging to useful cryptonetworks usually inflate in price over their lifetime, so earning them earlier gives miners more opportunity to profit from appreciation.

Difficulty

Ethereum and Bitcoin are self-regulating networks. As a network gets more popular, more mining hashpower joins in search of profits, and blocks might be found too quickly. To stay within range of its ideal 15-second block time, a dynamically self-adjusting value called *difficulty* will increase. If blocks are found too quickly or slowly, the system changes the difficulty to get within range of its ideal block time.

Generally speaking, *as time progresses, network difficulty increases.* However, the actual difficulty value is calculated with a formula that includes several variables. Network difficulty may decrease or go flat if miners begin to drop off the network or if overall hashpower decreases.[3]

After the Ethereum network experienced attacks in October and November 2016, the market price of ether dropped, and hashrate was reduced as miners who couldn't make a profit turned off their machines. It rose to its pre-attack highs several months later, commensurate with the recovery in the price of ether.

You can think of this difficulty variable as being part of the incentive structure to get miners on the network as soon as possible and to stay there. However, difficulty has another use in the EVM, as one of several factors used to determine a block's *score*, sometimes referred to as its *heaviness.* The heaviest, or highest-scoring, path through the transaction data structure can be said to be the longest, the one that most miners have historically converged upon as the true root-to-leaf path.

■ **Note**   In Ethereum and Bitcoin, the longest or heaviest chain is considered the canonical one. Each time the network finds a block, it selects the heaviest block with the highest score, and pays the miner who nominated it. This high score is the outcome for a block that is supported by the most proof of work.

---

[3]Ethereum Community Forum, "How Is Mining Difficulty Calculated," https://forum.ethereum.org/discussion/5002/how-is-the-mining-difficulty-calculated-on-ethereum, 2016.

Factors Required for Block Validation

Every candidate block that each individual miner constructs and seeks to validate contains four pieces of data:

> Hash of the transaction ledger for this block (as this machine heard about it)
>
> Root hash of the entire blockchain
>
> Block number since the chain started
>
> Difficulty of this block

If all these things check out, this block is a candidate for winning block. However, even with this information correct, the miner must still solve the proof-of-work algorithm. As you'll see, the algorithm is essentially a guessing game designed to take a certain amount of time, in service of the ideal 15-second block time.

When the guess is correct, this correct value, or *nonce*, is the final condition to render a block true, canonical, and valid. The nonce is known as evidence of solving the proof-of-work algorithm. Recall from Chapter 3 that blocks which are valid, but not the canonical winning block, are known as uncle blocks.

How Proof of Work Helps Regulate Block Time

Anyone who can optimize for the proof-of-work algorithm can find valid blocks faster, causing uncles to lag further and further behind. In the Bitcoin network, a small group of hardware companies has acquired a disproportionately huge amount of power over the network by creating hardware specifically built to run the Bitcoin PoW algorithm. The centralisation of mining efforts is highly profitable in Bitcoin, because it allows these big miners to find blocks faster, reaping all the block rewards. Slower machines never get a chance to solve a block, and eventually, even their uncle blocks come in further and further behind the winning block. In Ethereum, uncle blocks are required to bolster the winning block. As uncles lag more, it becomes harder for the network to find a true block, being that valid uncles are a requirement.

Enter the Ethash algorithm: The Ethereum protocol's defense against mining hardware optimization. Ethash is a derivative of Dagger-Hashimoto, which is a memory-hard algorithm that can't be brute-forced with a custom *application-specific integrated circuit (ASIC)*, like the kind that are popular with Bitcoin mining enterprises.

Key to this algorithm memory-hardness is its reliance on a *directed acyclic graph (DAG)* file, which is essentially a 1 GB dataset created anew every 125 hours, or 30,000 blocks. This period of 30,000 blocks is also known as an *epoch*.

Directed acyclic graph is a technical term for a tree in which each node is allowed to have multiple parents, with ten levels including the root, and a total of up to 225 values.

What's Going on with the DAG and Nonce?

In effect, each node is playing a guessing game with itself, trying to guess a nonce that will validate the current block; if it guesses the right nonce, it wins the block reward. If not, it continues guessing until it gets word that another node on the network has found a winner. Then, it discards the block it was mining downloads the new block, and begins mining a new block on top of *that one*. But the node gets both parameters of the guessing game, as well as a new pair of dice (so to speak) with each potential block as it rolls in. The rules of the guessing game are designed this way to prevent clever individual nodes from outsmarting the system in the pursuit of more mining rewards.

Therefore, you can think of the DAG file as a way of standardizing the *solution time* of the proof-of-work algorithm. It levels the playing field for miners, but more important, helps cluster block times around the 15-second mark by ensuring that—even with massive computing power—you can't guess the correct nonce a whole lot faster than your competitors.

All the data a node needs to participate in the guessing came is drawn from the blockchain itself. In cryptography, an encryption *seed* can be used to help generate a pseudorandom number, thus increasing the randomness of whatever encrypted output the Ethash algorithm produces. In Ethereum and Bitcoin, each node gets the seed from looking at the hash of the last known winning block. In this way, the node must be mining on the correct, canonical chain in order to play the game correctly. Performing proof of work on an erroneous block (say, an uncle) cannot yield a winning block. This is helpful if you're trying to reduce unfair advantage in a proof-of-work scheme, which could be used by a large pool of miners to highjack the network onto a version of the truth in which everyone's ether is transferred to the hijacker's accounts. Here is the process by which a node sets itself up to perform the PoW guessing game:

1. From an encryption seed derived from the block header, the mining node creates a 16 MB pseudorandom cache.

2. In turn, the cache is used to generate a larger 1 GB dataset that should be consistent from node to node; this is the DAG. This dataset grows over time, in a linear fashion, and is stored by all full nodes.

3. Guessing the nonce requires the machine to grab random slices of the DAG dataset and hash them together. This works similarly to using a salt with the hash function.

In cryptography, a random data chunk you toss into a one-way hash function is called a *salt*. Salts are like nonces: they make things more random, and thus more secure.

All This for Faster Blocks?

Believe it or not, all these modifications to the original Bitcoin paradigm were made in the service of faster block times. Block times as low as 3–5 seconds may be mathematically feasible.[4]

In both Bitcoin and Ethereum, we've said that block time is an idealized period for collecting transactions. Why is this? The system works to keep blocks as near as possible to the ideal, much the way that the human body tries to preserve homeostasis.

The Bitcoin protocol targets 10-minute block times, and Ethereum targets 15 seconds. Once a true block is found, it takes a short while for other nodes to find out about it. Up until they discard their orphan block and begin mining on the new one, they are actually competing against the new block instead of building upon it. Thus, the effort expended on the orphan is wasted. Think of it this way: if latency causes miners to hear about new blocks an average of one minute late, and new blocks come every 10 minutes, then the overall network is wasting roughly 10 percent of its haspower. Lengthening the time between blocks reduces this waste. In the opinion of some blockchain theorists, Satoshi Nakamoto chose this ratio because it seemed an acceptable level of waste. Ethereum's faster block time is desirable because it makes transactions confirm faster, but the Ethereum protocol has had to make provisions in its design for the commensurate decrease in security brought on by faster block times, as you'll see later in this chapter. Block time can be compared to *settlement time* in a securities trading, which in the United States, stands at three days after the trade date, also known as *T+3*. A proposal is under consideration by the SEC to quicken settlement time to *T+2*.

In Bitcoin, which has no smart-contract execution, blocks take a *theoretical* 10 minutes on average, but in reality, transactions process this quickly only about 63 percent of the time. About 13 percent of the time, it takes longer than 20 minutes for a transaction to receive a confirmation. During this time, it's possible to reverse a transaction up to 20 percent of the time.[5]

While merely irksome for Bitcoin enthusiasts and businesses, these conditions are unacceptable for a smart-contracts platform designed to power distributed software applications, so Ethereum takes a slightly different approach to mining, in order to achieve faster block times.

Making Fast Blocks Work

We've already discussed how faster block times are more desirable from the perspective of user experience. However, they can also produce undesirable effects.

Because nodes are located all over the world, it's hard for them to stay perfectly in sync. That's because information takes time to travel across the Internet from node to node, also known as *latency*. Although it may not seem like much time to humans, it's enough to create *collisions* in the transaction record where the books don't balance.

---

[4]Ethereum Blog, "Toward a 12-Second Block Time," `https://blog.ethereum.org/2014/07/11/toward-a-12-second-block-time/`, 2014.
[5]Ibid.

On average, it takes about 12 seconds for a transaction to propagate around the Ethereum or Bitcoin networks; in actuality, much of this time is consumed by the downloading of transactions to the node.[6] In the intervening time before it hears about a new block being found, a miner may continue to work on an old block briefly, before discarding it for the new winner. As described in the section above, uncles that receive mining effort after a valid block has already been found elsewhere in the network are also known as *stale* or *extinct* blocks.

Faster block times create a higher likelihood of stale blocks, and stale blocks decrease the network's absolute strength against attacks.[7] Worse yet, higher rates of stale blocks make it easier for mining pools to win increasing efficiency advantages over solo miners, consistently beating them out of mining rewards. At best, this is unfair, and at worst, it makes the network less expensive to attack.

■ **Note** Stale blocks are sometimes called *orphaned* blocks in Bitcoin, although this phraseology is confusing. These stale blocks do not have any blocks being built upon them—no child blocks—but they may have a perfectly valid block header. Thus, orphans do in fact have "parent" blocks.

How Ethereum Uses Stale Blocks

In Ethereum, as we've said already, orphans or stales have yet another name: they are called *uncles*, and they are counted toward the score, or *weight*, of a block. The way this is done in the Ethereum protocol is similar to the blockchain scoring system proposed in the GHOST protocol, which was outlined in a paper by Aviv Zhoar and Yonatan Sompolinsky in December 2013.

Vitalik Buterin describes the way he has adapted the GHOST idea for Ethereum, and how it compares to Bitcoin:

> *The idea is that even though stale blocks are not currently counted as part of the total weight of the chain, they could be; hence they propose a blockchain scoring system which takes stale blocks into account even if they are not part of the main chain. As a result, even if the main chain is only 50 percent efficient or even 5 percent efficient, an attacker attempting to pull off a 51 percent attack would still need to overcome the weight of the entire network. This, theoretically, solves the efficiency issue all the way down to 1-second block times. However, there is a problem: the protocol, as described, only includes stales in the scoring of a blockchain; it does not assign the stales a block reward.*

---

[6]Ibid.
[7]Ibid.

Uncle Rules and Rewards

The following are rules regarding uncles:

> In Ethereum's implementation of GHOST, uncles that are validated along with a block receive 7/8 of the static block reward, or 4.375 ether.[8]

> A maximum of two uncles are allowed per block.

> These two places are won on a first-come, first-served basis.

> No transaction fees are collected or paid out for uncle blocks, because users are paying these costs once already in the valid block, which actually executes their commands.

> Crucially, in order to be worthy of a reward, an uncle block must have *an ancestor in common with the true block within the last seven generations.*

This implementation of GHOST solves the issue of security loss by including uncle blocks in the calculation of which block has the largest total proof of work backing it. The uncle rewards are intended to solve the second issue, centralization, by paying miners who contribute to the security of the network, even if they do not nominate a winning block.

The Difficulty Bomb

It's worth mentioning that the GHOST protocol (even as Ethereum has adapted it) is the subject of some criticism. Although its flaws are known, they are generally regarded to be harmless. Fixing the GHOST implementation may not be worthwhile anyway, as it will be rendered deprecated when the Ethereum protocol moves away from a proof-of-work to what is known as a *proof-of-stake* consensus algorithm.[9]

One reason why cryptocurrencies have value in the marketplace is that they are limited in issuance. Today, 12.5 bitcoins are awarded per block (that is, every 10 minutes). This rate will continue until mid 2020, when 6.25 bitcoins per block will be awarded for each block. Rewards halve this way every four years until approximately the year 2110–40, when 21 million bitcoins will have been issued.

Ethereum achieves its limited issuance by planning to end the proof of work period entirely. The effective mining period for Ethereum will come to a close sometime in 2017–2018 when the Ethereum system makes the switch; one of the big selling points of proof of stake (or PoS) is that it does not require mining (and the accompanying energy expenditure) to reach consensus.

---

[8]GitHub, "Modified Ghost Implementation (Ethereum White Paper)," https://github.com/ethereum/wiki/wiki/White-Paper#modified-ghost-implementation, 2016.
[9]Bitslog, "Uncle Mining: an Ethereum Protocol Flaw," https://bitslog.wordpress.com/2016/04/28/uncle-mining-an-ethereum-consensus-protocol-flaw/, 2016.

In an effort to force this transition, and simultaneously limit the issuance period for ether, the core developers have built in a *difficulty bomb* that makes proof-of-work mining less and less feasible beginning in the latter half of 2017, before finally becoming impossible in 2021.[10]

How this new proof-of-stake system will work is the subject of much research and debate within the community. To read more about the research being done in this area, skip to Chapter 11.

Miner's Winning Payout Structure

A successful miner of a winning block receives a flat payment, plus transaction fees, plus a share of the bounty of all uncles that helped it win. Thus it can be said the rewards in the Ethereum protocol are determined as follows:

1. A set block reward of 5.0 ether (for the miner that finds the winning block)

2. Fee payments of the gas expended within the block (for the miner that finds the winning block)

3. 1/32 ether per uncle of this block (for miners that find uncles)

Limits on Ancestry

The part of the protocol requiring uncles to be within seven blocks of the winning block to receive a partial award exists to make block history "forgettable" after a small number of blocks. The number seven was picked because it offers a reasonable amount of time for a miner to find an uncle, but not so long that it imposes centralization risks.

The Block Processing Play by Play

In order to escape uncle-hood and become the heaviest block, a true block (sometimes called a *nephew*) needs to pass muster with a long series of steps used in the processing of each block. An important component of this process is the block validator algorithm. This algorithm seeks to validate the hash that comes with the block, located in the block's header. This aspect of block processing makes a good on-ramp to the anatomy of a block as a data object.

■ **Note** In programming, data structures often have a header containing certain essential information that the computer must read first. Just as in human word processors, the *header* is merely the top of a body of text. In this analogy, the body of text is the block data structure.

---

[10]StackOverflow, "When Will the Difficulty Bomb Make Mining Impossible?" http://ethereum. stackexchange.com/questions/3779/when-will-the-difficulty-bomb-make-mining-impossible/3819#3819, 2016.

Before a completed block can undergo processing and acceptance by the rest of the network, and before nodes can begin mining on top of a new block, each and every node must independently download and validate the block before begining to mine in top of it. Here are all the steps the block validator algorithm takes, in order:

1. Check if the previous block referenced exists and is valid.

2. Check that the timestamp of the block is greater than that of the referenced previous block and less than 15 minutes into the future.

3. Check that the block number, difficulty, transaction root, uncle root and gas limit (various low-level Ethereum-specific concepts) are valid.

4. Check that the nonce on the block is valid, showing the evidence of proof of work.

5. Apply all transactions in this now-validated block to the EVM state. If any errors are thrown, or if total gas exceeds the GASLIMIT, return an error and roll back the state change.

6. Add the block reward to the final state change.

7. Check that the Merkle tree root final state is equal to the final state root in the block header.

Only after these seven steps is a block canonized as valid and true!

Why all this fuss about the block header? To make a blockchain, it would be theoretically possible to create block headers that directly contain data about every transaction, but this would pose scalability challenges and require immensely powerful hardware to run a node.[11]

In Bitcoin and Ethereum, a data structure called a *Merkle tree* is used to avoid putting every single transaction in the header, which would be large and unwieldy. Ethereum adds a data structure representing the state of the EVM, called a state tree. Global state is presented in an Ethereum block by another tree structure known as a *Patricia tree*. These tree structures are the subject of the next section.

Evaluating the Ancestry of Blocks and Transactions

To understand what's in a block header, and why the contents of the block header are important to determining the longest, heaviest chain, you need to take a step back and explore how computers store data—and how they go about changing that data once stored.

First and foremost, the role of tree structures is to help the node verify the data it receives inside blocks, such as the transaction ledger. Secondarily, their role is to do this fast, so that computers of all shapes and sizes can read the blockchain quickly.

---

[11]Ethereum Blog, "Merkling in Ethereum," https://blog.ethereum.org/2015/11/15/merkling-in-ethereum/, 2015.

In computer science, an *associative array* (or *dictionary*) refers to a collection of (key/value) pairs. Recall the concept of key/value pairs from the discussion of data objects in Chapter 1. In an associative array, the association between keys and values can be changed. This association is called a *binding*.

Operations associated with dictionaries include the following:

Adding key/value pairs to the collection

Removing pairs from the collection

Modifying existing pairs

Looking up a value associated with a given key

Hash tables, search trees, and other specialized tree structures are common solutions to the *dictionary problem*, where a dictionary is a generic term for a database of records. Solving dictionary problems involves methodologies for querying for a key (a word) and calling up its value (a definition).

How Ethereum and Bitcoin Use Trees

In mathematics, a *tree* is an ordered data structure used to store an associative array of keys and values. A *radix tree* is a variant that is compressed, requiring less memory. In a normal radix tree, each character in the key describes a path through the data structure to get to the corresponding value, like a set of directions.

Creating a *Merkle tree* requires hashing a large number of "chunks" of transaction data together until they become only one: a *root hash*. In Ethereum and Bitcoin, the Merkle tree structure is used to record the transaction ledger in each block. The root for the Merkle tree is hashed in with other metadata and included in the header of the subsequent block. Thus, it can be said that each additional transaction (within each block) irrevocably changes the Merkle root; even one wrong transaction will make the root hash look completely different and thus, obviously wrong. This is how blocks can prove their legitimate ancestry to the block validator algorithm, which is part of the overall block processing routine.

For a Bitcoin client, determining the status of a single transaction is as easy as looking at the header of the most recent block of the main chain. There, the client should find the Merkle proof showing that the root hash for the block contains the transaction in one of its Merkle trees. The Merkle root is a fingerprint of all the transactions, correctly ordered, that have occurred in the blockchain up until that block.

Merkle-Patricia Trees

Thanks to the block header, it's quick and easy for a node to look for, read, or verify block data. In Bitcoin, the block header is an 80-byte chunk of data that includes the Merkle root as well as five other things. The Bitcoin block header contains:

A hash of the previous block header

A timestamp

A mining difficulty value

A proof-of-work nonce

A root hash for the Merkle tree containing the transactions for that block

Merkle trees are ideal for storing transaction ledgers, but that's about it. From the perspective of the EVM, one limitation of the Merkle tree is that although it can prove or disprove the inclusion of transactions in the root hash, it can't prove or query the current state of the network, such as a given user's account holdings.

Contents of an Ethereum Block Header

To remedy this shortcoming and allow the EVM to run stateful contracts, every block header in Ethereum contains not just one Merkle (transaction) tree, but *three* trees for three kinds of objects:

Transaction tree

Receipts tree (data showing the outcome of each transaction)

State tree

To make this possible, the Ethereum protocol combines the Merkle tree with the other tree structure we described above, the Patricia tree. This tree structure is fully deterministic: two Patricia trees with the same (key/value) bindings will always have the same root hash, providing increased efficiency for common database operations such as inserts, lookups, and deletes.[12] It is therefore possible for Ethereum clients to get verifiable answers to all sorts of queries it makes to the network, such as the following:

Has transaction *X* been included in block? (Handled by the transaction tree.)

Tell me all instances of event *Y* in the last 30 days. (Handled by the receipts tree.)

What is the current balance of contract account *Z*? (Handled by the state tree.)

For more about how these tree structures work and why they were chosen, check out `http://trees.eth.guide`.

Forking

As discussed earlier in this chapter, a network of miners may split in two, if they cannot agree on the longest, heaviest chain. There's much ado about forking in the cryptocurrency community, where it seems to imply the fracture of a community of humans along with a loss of consensus in the machine network.

---

[12]Ethereum Wiki, "Merkle Patricia Tree Specification," `https://github.com/ethereum/wiki/wiki/Patricia-Tree#merkle-patricia-tree-specification`, 2016.

In reality, nascent forks are constantly happening. Sometimes one branch dies, sometimes both die, and sometimes one lives on to propagate a winning nephew block. A *fork* occurs when two valid blocks point to the same parent, but some of the miners see one, and the rest see the other. Effectively, this creates two versions of "the truth," ensuring that these two groups can no longer be said to be on the same network.

▧ **Note**   A state fork is a much bigger deal than a protocol fork. In a *protocol fork*, no data is changed, but miners may adjust parameters or update code on their nodes to make them perform to a modified specification that the community has agreed is an overall improvement. Protocol forks can thus be said to be voluntary, whereas state forks are not necessarily so.

In Ethereum, these constant budding forks are resolved within four blocks, as a matter of mathematical certainty, as one chain finds a winner, gets longer, and begins to "pull" other nodes toward it with the incentive of not only the miner fee for finding and executing the correct block, but all the added incentive of collecting the uncle block rewards.

Sometimes a node will find the "right" chain after already receiving a reward for about one to three blocks. Once the node jumps to a better, longer, more winning chain, that mining reward may disappear. However, this all happens within four blocks—that is, one minute—so these small errata are considered no big deal.

Deliberate forks are typically deployed by attackers in order to *double-spend* funds: to make money out of thin air by simultaneously sending one balance to many accounts.

In fact, anyone with more than 50 percent of the hashpower can engender a "hostile" deliberate fork, so to speak. In a *double spend attack*, an attacker operating a fleet of miners, with a large amount of hashpower, sends an ether transaction to purchase a product. After getting hold of the product, the attacker puts together an erroneous block with a second transaction. This second transaction attempts to send the same funds back to the attacker. He or she then creates a block at the same level as the block which contained the original transaction, but containing the second transaction instead, and dedicates all possible hashpower to mining on the fork. Should the attacker have more than 50 percent of haspower, the double spend is guaranteed to succeed eventually at any block depth. Below 50 percent it's far less prone to succeed. But this attack is still feared enough that, in practice, most exchanges and other institutions who use ether wait for several confirmations before considering the transfer complete.

Mining Tutorial

Mining is a great excuse to try Geth. Because Geth is such a great tool for learning, and because it's fairly easy to install, this section provides installation instructions for macOS, Windows, and Ubuntu.

Installing Geth on macOS

First, open the Terminal on your Mac, located in the Applications folder. Then, type the following at the command line:

```
brew update
brew upgrade
```

Once updating is complete, and the command line returns, type the following:

```
brew tap ethereum/ethereum
brew install ethereum
```

Installing Geth on Windows

Download the latest stable binary. Extract geth.exe from zip, open a command Terminal and type this:

```
chdir <path to extracted binary>
open geth.exe
```

Getting Comfortable with the Command Line

After you install Geth on Ubuntu (described next), you'll proceed right into some exercises. These exercises assume the use of macOS or Ubuntu Terminal applications. Windows Geth commands will not be discussed here, but can be found at http://clients.eth.guide.

The following guide is written for people who may be using the command line for the first time. If this is you, then you should notice a few things right away.

When you first open your Terminal application, located in the Applications folder on macOS and Ubuntu, you'll see a blinking cursor. This indicates the computer is ready to receive instructions.

Installing Geth on Ubuntu 14.04

To install Geth on Ubuntu, first open the Terminal and type this, then hit Enter:

```
sudo apt-get install software-properties-common
```

One caveat to this installation, depending on hardware configuration, is that some Ubuntu users may need to install a font library, or the Geth installation will throw an error. You can find this library at https://community.linuxmint.com/software/view/ttf-ancient-fonts or clients.eth.guide. The error is shown in Figure 6-1.

```
You might want to run 'apt-get -f install' to correct these:
The following packages have unmet dependencies:
 bootnode:i386 : Depends: ttf-ancient-fonts:i386 but it is not installable
E: Unmet dependencies. Try 'apt-get -f install' with no packages (or specify a s
olution).
```

Figure 6-1. *Some Ubuntu users may get this error*

Simply install this font package and things should go smoothly.
Then type the following:

```
sudo add-apt-repository -y ppa:ethereum/ethereum
```

The program will ask you to type your password. It may not appear on the screen, or even look like anything is being entered at all, but ignore that and press Enter. You should see a result similar to Figure 6-2.

```
ubie@ubie-M11AD: ~
ubie@ubie-M11AD:~$ sudo add-apt-repository -y ppa:ethereum/ethereum
[sudo] password for ubie:
gpg: keyring `/tmp/tmpdc6264j7/secring.gpg' created
gpg: keyring `/tmp/tmpdc6264j7/pubring.gpg' created
gpg: requesting key 923F6CA9 from hkp server keyserver.ubuntu.com
gpg: /tmp/tmpdc6264j7/trustdb.gpg: trustdb created
gpg: key 923F6CA9: public key "Launchpad PPA for Ethereum" imported
gpg: Total number processed: 1
gpg:               imported: 1  (RSA: 1)
OK
ubie@ubie-M11AD:~$ 
```

Figure 6-2. *Enter your password to complete installation, and you'll see this result*

Putting sudo in front of a Terminal command to execute commands as the root user, or most the most powerful user role in the Unix architecture, with access to all files and commands. Next, at the prompt, type this and hit Enter:

```
sudo apt-get update
```

And then type this and hit Enter:

```
sudo apt-get install ethereum
```

Enter your computer's administrator password, probably the one you use to login to your computer after it boots up. When the program asks whether you'd like to allow the installation to take some hard drive space, type Y (for yes) and press Enter.

Next, let's run Geth. After installation is finished, you can start Geth by typing its name at the command prompt:

```
geth
```

You'll see some code whizz by, looking like Figure 6-3.

```
I1110 13:05:52.118503 ethdb/database.go:83] Alloted 16MB cache and 16 file handl
es to /home/ubie/.ethereum/dapp
I1110 13:05:52.463738 eth/backend.go:172] Protocol Versions: [63 62], Network Id
: 1
I1110 13:05:52.466176 eth/backend.go:201] Blockchain DB Version: 3
I1110 13:05:52.706356 core/blockchain.go:214] Last header: #1747389 [e5268893..]
TD=2965298570275883415θ
I1110 13:05:52.706385 core/blockchain.go:215] Last block: #1747389 [e5268893..] T
D=29652985702758834150
I1110 13:05:52.706396 core/blockchain.go:216] Fast block: #1747389 [e5268893..] T
D=29652985702758834150
I1110 13:05:52.776676 p2p/server.go:313] Starting Server
I1110 13:05:52.782759 p2p/nat/nat.go:111] mapped network port udp:30303 -> 30303
 (ethereum discovery) using NAT-PMP(192.168.1.1)
I1110 13:05:53.095713 p2p/discover/udp.go:217] Listening, enode://a7cca350a5b279
c131b80d2673d336dce1e46749a00cecd0b87550bc7f45222b46e1352d41da878c79780c0a54e3e0
c56dc6c6b60c9cf82155c7a57c0476f084066.65.50.108:30303
I1110 13:05:53.096596 node/node.go:296] IPC endpoint opened: /home/ubie/.ethereu
m/geth.ipc
I1110 13:05:53.096706 p2p/server.go:556] Listening on [::]:30303
I1110 13:05:53.102656 p2p/nat/nat.go:111] mapped network port tcp:30303 -> 30303
 (ethereum p2p) using NAT-PMP(192.168.1.1)
I1110 13:05:56.250622 eth/downloader/downloader.go:319] Block synchronisation st
arted
I1110 13:06:00.969563 core/blockchain.go:1001] imported 1 block(s) (0 queued 0 i
gnored) including 0 txs in 2.760345141s. #1747390 [de9c4dce / de9c4dce]
I1110 13:06:06.740200 core/blockchain.go:1001] imported 3 block(s) (0 queued 0 i
gnored) including 9 txs in 5.770474253s. #1747393 [f75204e1 / f499207c]
```

Figure 6-3. *Geth is synchronizing*

This will go on forever if you let it. Press Control+C to get the synchronization to stop, and you'll be dropped back at your same old command-line prompt. You have now exited Geth.

So what's happening here? Geth is not mining, but it is synchronizing itself with the blockchain by downloading past blocks. It does this in order to show you an up-to-date balance on your accounts, and to quickly send and receive transactions, just like Mist. In fact, Mist does this synchronization thing too, remember? It looks like Figure 6-4.

Figure 6-4. *When Geth synchronizes, it's performing the same operation you see in the Mist wallet, pictured here*

However, Geth is fairly dumb; it can do only one thing at a time: synchronize. You can't run any EVM code from here. To gain some control, you'll need to take advantage of Geth's built-in JavaScript console, which allows you to execute commands directly in the EVM via the Terminal on your computer. How cool is that?

Executing Commands in the EVM via the Geth Console

You can use Geth commands in the Terminal to execute many essential functions on the Ethereum network. The formula for Geth commands is:

```
geth [options] command [command options] [arguments...]
```

And you can find a full list of commands, options, and arguments at https://github.com/ethereum/go-ethereum/wiki/Command-Line-Options. However, since the ultimate promise of the Ethereum network is truly distributed apps, we'll focus on using the Ethereum JavaScript API through a console you can open up in Geth. The console is really a *JSRE*, or *JavaScript Runtime Environment* that operates inside of Geth. Ethereum's JSRE exposes the full Web3.js JavaScript dapp API, which is covered more in Chapter 8. The JSRE can be used actively (in the console) or non-interactively (with written scripts).

In addition to the dapp API, Geth also supports a whole slew of management APIs for remote management of your Ethereum note. An example is the personal and admin APIs, which exposes a method for access the file system, execute commands, and monitor your node remotely. These APIs and follow the same conventions as used in the dapp API. You can learn more about the management API at: https://github.com/ethereum/go-ethereum/wiki/JavaScript-Console#management-apis.

128

▓ **Note**   That running Geth and Mist at the same time will cause an error. A node can run only one network daemon per machine.

To restart Geth with the console, type the following:

```
geth console
```

If you already have Mist running and synchronized, you can tell Geth to use Mist's node to connect by starting Geth via the following command. This saves you from having to wait for Geth to sync all over again if your machine already has most of the blockchain stored locally:

```
geth attach
```

You can call `console` and `attach` one after the other. Why is this useful? You can begin using the JavaScript console in Geth right away if you have a fully synchronized Mist client running. That doesn't matter much for now, but if you were sending and receiving real transactions to the public blockchain with Geth, you might need to wait for it to synchronize before your balance queries are returned correctly.

Below, we'll use some JavaScript API calls in the console. A full guide to these calls is here: https://github.com/ethereum/go-ethereum/wiki/JavaScript-Console. Next, we'll learn how to work with accounts and balances by calling some JavaScript methods interactively. To learn more about using the JSRE non-interactively, visit https://github.com/ethereum/go-ethereum/wiki/JavaScript-Console#non-interactive-use-jsre-script-mode.

▓ **Note**   These Geth commands connect to the main network. Recall that the testnet has fake ether you can use to test, whereas the main network requires you to buy ether on an exchange. Mining it is not an easy way to get ahold of ether these days, but we're going to try it anyway for fun.

Your Geth client should be running with the console enabled, giving you a command prompt. Let's create an account by using a JavaScript API call. In your head, choose a password. In the console, type this, then hit Enter:

```
personal.newAccount("your_new_account_password_here")
```

Replace the text between the quotes with the password you chose. Your primary account is account 0 by default. You will be returned a public key, in green type, as pictured in Figure 6-5.

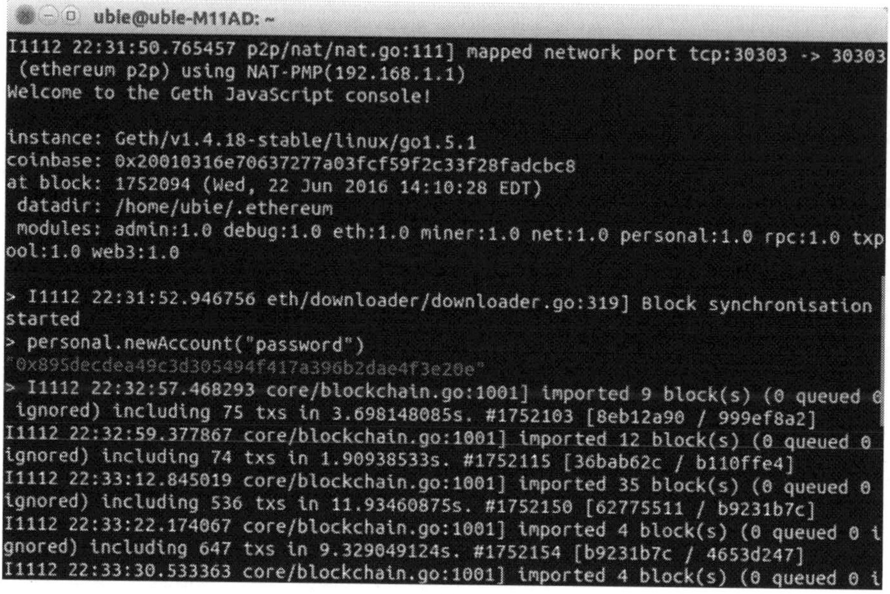

Figure 6-5. *Creating a new account in the JavaScript console couldn't be easier. Your new public key appears in green. Don't forget your password!*

You can check out all your accounts in the console by typing the following:

```
personal.listAccounts
```

No doubt the balance will return zero. But, no matter: the private key for this new account will be stored with the other private keys you create, in the very same directory you looked at in Chapter 2; any value you add here will be backed up when you back up the rest of your private keys. To review the process for doing so, go to the following:

```
http://backup.eth.guide
```

Recall at the beginning of this section, with the description of the Geth JSRE as the gateway to the Ethereum JavaScript API. This API is part of the Web3.js library, which must be installed on your machine for you to take advantage of many of the commands. It is available as an Node Package Manager (npm) module, a Meteor.js package, and in other forms. You can learn more about this library at https://github.com/ethereum/web3.js/. For a complete listing of JavaScript Dapp API calls, check out http://js.eth.guide or see the Ethereum JavaScript API at

```
https://github.com/ethereum/wiki/wiki/JavaScript-API.
```

For developers with pre-existing JavaScript skills, the JS console in Geth may be more intuitive than writing Solidity scripts using the global varables and functions we described in Chapter 4. The web3 object provides access to all sorts of methods that will feel familiar to JavaScript developers. Spend some time perusing the console wiki to get an idea of the kinds of scripts you could run locally on your machine, in order to automate actions taken in Geth. Next, you'll learn how to get on the testnet with Geth, and finally, you'll start up your miner on the main network and even attempt to mine a block with your own custom signature on it.

Launching Geth with Flags

Another popular way to get things done at the Geth command line is to launch Geth with certain flags. A full list of options, and their corresponding flags, are located here: https://github.com/ethereum/go-ethereum/wiki/Command-Line-Options.

To start Geth on the testnet, type this:

```
geth --testnet
```

You'll see text output similar to the screen in Figure 6-6, except that this mining is taking place on the testnet. Press Control+C to stop it.

```
⬤ ⊖ ⬚  ubie@uble-M11AD: ~
I1112 21:59:01.211092 core/blockchain.go:216] Fast block: #1840762 [061c88f3…] T
D=400999452729270
I1112 21:59:01.213422 p2p/server.go:313] Starting Server
I1112 21:59:01.220354 p2p/nat/nat.go:111] mapped network port udp:30303 -> 30303
 (ethereum discovery) using NAT-PMP(192.168.1.1)
I1112 21:59:01.240635 p2p/discover/udp.go:217] Listening, enode://6d82ab2152ed2a
072fceaab82d000a51cdde18046b049961673f4e97c1d81ca2d25fc87ba84b0a44d46ced172b167e
2ea0d5549026db546cf475c66d987429df@66.65.50.108:30303
I1112 21:59:01.242361 p2p/server.go:556] Listening on [::]:30303
I1112 21:59:01.243053 node/node.go:296] IPC endpoint opened: /home/ubie/.ethereu
m/testnet/geth.ipc
I1112 21:59:01.248442 p2p/nat/nat.go:111] mapped network port tcp:30303 -> 30303
 (ethereum p2p) using NAT-PMP(192.168.1.1)
^CI1112 21:59:03.081600 cmd/utils/cmd.go:81] Got interrupt, shutting down...
I1112 21:59:03.081775 node/node.go:328] IPC endpoint closed: /home/ubie/.ethereu
m/testnet/geth.ipc
I1112 21:59:03.081814 core/blockchain.go:578] Chain manager stopped
I1112 21:59:03.081828 eth/handler.go:225] Stopping ethereum protocol handler...
I1112 21:59:03.081862 eth/handler.go:246] Ethereum protocol handler stopped
I1112 21:59:03.081964 core/tx_pool.go:172] Transaction pool stopped
I1112 21:59:03.082018 eth/backend.go:500] Automatic pregeneration of ethash DAG
OFF (ethash dir: /home/ubie/.ethash)
I1112 21:59:03.082286 ethdb/database.go:176] closed db:/home/ubie/.ethereum/test
net/chaindata
```

Figure 6-6. *Output from testnet*

For quick access to the CLI options, this short link is also available: http://cli.eth.guide.

As of this writing, network difficulty is fairly high, and solo miners might take a very long time to find a block. But in the next section, we'll start mining to our new wallet address anyway, to understand the experience of the miners who secure the network.

Fire Up Your Miner!

Geth does not begin mining automatically; you will give it the command to start or stop mining. In these examples, you will be mining with your machine's CPU. Mining with a GPU is more effective, but slightly more complicated, and is more suitable for specialized mining rigs anyway. We'll discuss these later in the chapter.

To begin mining on the main network, open a new Terminal window and enter the JavaScript console by typing the following:

```
geth console
```

You'll see the node begin to synchronize, but it will quickly return a command-line prompt where you can enter commands as Geth works in the background, so to speak.

▓ **Note** In the console, don't worry if the output text from mining or synchronization appears to overwrite your commands; it just appears that way. When you press Enter in the console, your command will be executed as normal, even if it seems to have broken onto several lines.

In order to get paid, you'll need to tell your node the Ethereum address for receiving your mining payments. Remember that because the EVM is a global virtual machine, it doesn't care whether the Ethereum address, or public key, you enter was created, or is currently associated with, your local computer. Everything is local to the EVM.

To set your etherbase as the recipient address for your payout, type this command in the console:

```
miner.setEtherbase(eth.accounts[your_address_here])
```

To finally begin mining, type this:

```
miner.start()
```

Boom! Your miner will begin. In the off-chance you find a block, your payment will be received at the address you set above, but don't be surprised if it takes days or even weeks. You'll see the node generating the DAG file and beginning the mining process, as shown in Figure 6-7. Why isn't ether mining an instant money-maker? That has a lot to do with your hardware, as you'll see below.

```
● ◉ ◎  ubie@ubie-M11AD: ~
I1112 22:03:26.071880 eth/backend.go:454] Automatic pregeneration of ethash DAG
ON (ethash dir: /home/ubie/.ethash)
true
> I1112 22:03:26.072245 eth/backend.go:461] checking DAG (ethash dir: /home/ubie
/.ethash)
I1112 22:03:26.072435 miner/worker.go:539] commit new work on block 1748011 with
 0 txs & 0 uncles. Took 623.351µs
I1112 22:03:26.072570 ethash.go:259] Generating DAG for epoch 58 (size 156027865
6) (8f602dc7d86df0a7c8e7467ec0d211062ee85c5c14c6d2f6c025976cf550e8c5)
I1112 22:03:27.548451 ethash.go:291] Generating DAG: 0%
I1112 22:03:33.584568 ethash.go:291] Generating DAG: 1%
I1112 22:03:39.798725 ethash.go:291] Generating DAG: 2%
I1112 22:03:45.891413 ethash.go:291] Generating DAG: 3%
> I1112 22:03:51.758028 ethash.go:291] Generating DAG: 4%
> I1112 22:03:53.465117 eth/downloader/downloader.go:319] Block synchronisation
started
I1112 22:03:53.465561 miner/miner.go:75] Mining operation aborted due to sync op
eration
> I1112 22:03:57.340299 eth/downloader/downloader.go:298] Synchronisation failed
: receipt download canceled (requested)
```

Figure 6-7. *The miner gets ready to mine*

You can stop this process by typing the following:

```
miner.stop()
```

Next, you'll put a personal tag on the blocks you mine, just because.

EXERCISE: ADD YOUR NAME TO THE BLOCKCHAIN

Using the JavaScript console, you can add extra data—a grand total of 32 bytes, or enough to write some plain text or enter some ciphertext for someone else to read.

In the console, your miner should be stopped. Now type this JavaScript command with your name or a message between the quotes:

```
miner.setExtra("My_message_here")
```

Then type this:

```
miner.start()
```

The console will return true and begin mining. Should you find a block, it will be marked with your signature, which you can view on any blockchain explorer such as Etherchain (https://etherchain.org).

EXERCISE: CHECK YOUR BALANCE

Install the Web3.js library (https://github.com/ethereum/wiki/wiki/
JavaScript-API#adding-web3) as described in the last section, to try out some
of the Ethereum JavaScript API calls. These include checking a balance, sending
a transaction, creating an account, and all sorts of other mathematical and
blockchain-related functions. If your etherbase private key is held on your machine,
for example, you can get the balance by typing in the console:

```
eth.getBalance(eth.coinbase).toNumber();
```

Hopefully by now, you have a working understanding of mining, and you've see it
happen before your own eyes. In reality, the most effective way to see how mining
moves state transition forward, executing contracts, is to work with the testnet.

Mining on the Testnet

One quick final note about mining. Recall in Chapter 5 that the Mist wallet can mine on
the testnet, but not the main net. Why is this?

Actually, there is no need for Mist to mine on the main net and take up your
computer's resources, because your contracts will execute without you mining. This is
because there are currently thousands of nodes already mining on the public Ethereum
chain, and being paid real ether to do so.

▓ **Note** If your contracts aren't executing on the testnet, don't go berserk! Turn your Mist
or Geth testnet miner on, and your contracts will execute. This is a common mistake.

While there may coincidentally be others mining on the testnet while you are testing your
contracts, there may also not be. Because there's no real financial incentive to leave a miner
running on the testnet, you might find yourself in a lull, with nobody else on the testnet. This
is why Mist allows testnet mining along with its GUI contract deployment interface.

GPU Mining Rigs

Most ether mining is done with specialized GPU miners like the ones in Figure 6-8, which
are operated by me. Two of the machines pictured are running the Claymore Dualminer,
a custom mining program written by a Bitcointalk.org forum member named Claymore,
and which mines both ether and another cryptocurrency simultaneously on multi-GPU
rigs. You can learn more about the Claymore Dualminer at https://bitcointalk.org/
index.php?topic=1433925.0.

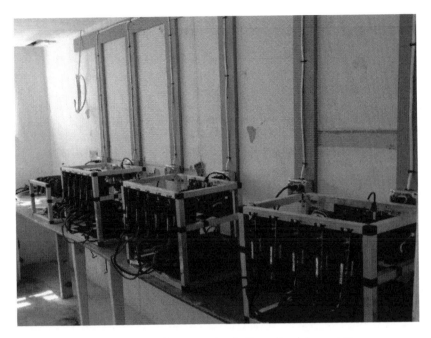

Figure 6-8. *Four Ethereum miners running in the author's basement*

The third and fourth rigs pictured here are running ethOS, a special Linux distro specifically created for rigs mining Ethereum, Zcash, or Monero. This is a far easier solution if you're building from scratch. You can learn more about ethOS at http://ethosdistro.com.

Several software patches are available for Windows, macOS, and Ubuntu that enable multi-GPU mining. However, this is easiest done on Ubuntu.

If you're running Ubuntu and you'd like to mine with multiple GPUs, it's easiest done with AMD hardware. Once your video cards are physically installed, a few quick commands are all that are needed. In Ubuntu 14.04, open your Terminal and type the following:

```
sudo apt-get -y update
sudo apt-get -y upgrade -f
sudo apt-get install fglrx-updates
sudo amdconfig --adapter=all --initial
```

Then reboot. Next, enable OpenCL by entering the following Terminal commands:

```
export GO_OPENCL=true
export GPU_MAX_ALLOC_PERCENT=100
export GPU_SINGLE_ALLOC_PERCENT=100
```

You can check that the configuration worked correctly by opening the Terminal back up again and typing this:

```
aticonfig --list-adapters
```

135

You should now see your AMD graphics cards in a list. The card denoted with an asterix (*) is the computer's default video output. If you see a black screen, your monitor may be plugged into the wrong video card.

Mining on a Pool with Multiple GPUs

It may be a little bit late to get serious about mining for profit. The outset of this chapter covered the concept of network difficulty. As we've discussed already, network difficulty is already quite high, and the effective mining period for Ethereum will end sometime in 2017 or 2018. Competition for mining rewards is intense. You can think of your miner's chances of finding a winning block as being represented by the ratio of your miner's hashing power to network difficulty. People who are mining for profit seek to gain an edge by using powerful hardware to improve their chances.

As Ethereum becomes more popular, time passes, and mining hashpower on the network increases, mining becomes less and less appealing for most users. However, it can still be fun and useful to learn how Ethereum mining works, if for no other reason than to mine new cryptocurrencies in the future. If you have hardware accessible, there's no reason not to experiment with mining, even if buying ether outright may be cheaper than mining it in some localities.

There are several mining pools, as you'll see if you visit http://mining.eth.guide, but for simplicity's sake we'll use a program called QtMiner for Ubuntu 14.04, which you can download from http://ethpool.org/downloads/qtminer2.tgz.

Once downloaded, extract the archive and make the qt.miner script executable:

```
tar zxvf qtminer.tgz
cd ./qtminer
chmod +x qtminer.sh
```

Finally, start QTMiner with the following command, where *address* is the Ethereum address you want to be paid mining rewards, and *name* is the name of this particular mining rig:

```
./qtminer.sh -s us1.ethermine.org:4444 -u address.name -G
```

To check your earnings without opening Mist, which can take forever to sync, go to Ethermine.org and enter the same Ethereum address you included previously in the upper-right search box.

Summary

In this chapter you've tackled the most complex facet of the Ethereum protocol: the mining process. You learned how miners are paid, how much, and how the system ensures that no single mining pool with advanced equipment can dominate the network. You installed Geth and began executing JavaScript methods at the command line. You started small with testnet mining, and moved all the way up to multi-GPU mining on a pool. If you'd like to see a dynamic picture of all these factors at work in the live chain, visit `https://ethstats.net`.

Let's integrate what you've learned in this chapter into the prior chapters with a short summary from end to end:

A block in Ethereum is a record of transactions that transpire over a given 12 to 15-second interval. Each time a node synchronizes with the network, it downloads blocks from nearby nodes, before assembling them into a data structure that allows the root hash to be computed and verified. Thus, it can trust it has an accurate history of the blockchain, and it can safely begin mining new blocks or sending new transactions. This is the synchronization process you glimpsed when installing Mist and Geth.

In the next chapter, you'll learn about the economic incentives and disincentives that make proof-of-work mining so resilient against attacks. This emerging field is known as *cryptoeconomics*.

CHAPTER 7

■ ■ ■

Cryptoeconomics Survey

The study of economic activity conducted across secure computer networks is known as cryptoeconomics

Let's take a break from mining and deployment and talk about some of the design choices that went into Ethereum: specifically, those around its system of economic incentives and disincentives. Broadly speaking, this facet of Ethereum overlaps with the field of *game theory*, the study of rational, intelligent decision-making in situations involving conflict and cooperation.

Game theory is used in economics, defense planning, psychology, political science, biology, and even the study of gambling (!) as a methodology for studying, analyzing, and predicting the behavior of humans and computers working inside a known system.

This book is about understanding the purpose of the Ethereum network, and how to get connected to it. We're fortunate that we don't have to be mathematicians to do so. If you happen to be one, and you'd like a more technical explanation of the concepts in this brief but important chapter, consult the Ethereum White Paper and Yellow Paper, located at the following URLs, respectively:

- https://github.com/ethereum/wiki/wiki/White-Paper
- http://gavwood.com/paper.pdf

How We Got Here

Ciphers have existed in one way or another for thousands of years as a way of sending coded messages, but the study of cryptography became formalized as a discipline only within the decades since World War II. During that war, Allied powers were able to intercept and crack enciphered messages transmitted in Morse code by the Axis powers *Enigma machine*, a factor that General Dwight D. Eisenhower considered decisive in the Allied victory.[1]

---

[1] F.W. Winterbotham, The Ultra Secret: The Inside Story of Operation Ultra, Bletchley Park and Enigma (London: Orion Publishers, 2000).

© Chris Dannen 2017
C. Dannen, *Introducing Ethereum and Solidity*, DOI 10.1007/978-1-4842-2535-6_7

Today, with digital communications, we don't have to rely on transmission over the fuzzy analog radio spectrum, where information can fade in and out with the hiss and jumble of interference. We get crisp, clear, digital signals across many devices and protocols. The digital communication age we know today was ushered in by *cryptanalysis*, also known as *code-breaking*. The new field of *information theory* that resulted from it made modern computers, computer languages, and networking into reality, decades after they were envisioned by futurist inventors.

New Technologies Create New Economies

The great promise of information theory is certainty and privacy. Ones and zeros allow computers to send signals that are unmistakable; we can trust computers to execute the same code the same way each time, thus enabling the high degree of automation we enjoy today. Cryptography makes it possible to keep the meaning of those signals private to the sender and recipient, even when messages travel across the globe, riding along many networks along the way—some of which may be equipped with a spying apparatus.

To secure the information they send across networks, today's computers can encrypt information with far greater strength than the Enigma machine circa 1945. *Cryptographic messaging* can be loosely defined as communication in an untrustworthy environment, or under any circumstances where your information is prone to exploitation or destruction. War is one example, but so are industrial espionage, religious persecution, or even natural disasters.

The field of economics typically studies interactions between people, sometimes in hostile contexts such as war. The emerging field of *cryptoeconomics* is the study of economic activity conducted across network protocols in an adversarial environment.

The domains of cryptoeconomics include the following:

- Online trust
- Online reputation
- Cryptographically secure communication
- Decentralized applications
- Currency or assets as a web service (so to speak)
- Peer-to-peer financial contracts (smart contracts)
- Network database consensus protocols
- Antispam and anti-Sybil attack algorithms

In a Sybil attack, an attacker floods a peer-to-peer network with a large number of pseudonymous identities, in order to gain a disproportionately large influence. This is a noteworthy vulnerability for peer-to-peer networks. The 51-percent attack described in Chapter 6 is similar to a Sybil attack. As you'll see, most of what you might call *applied cryptoeconomics* is creating a game-like system with workable incentives and disincentives, which create a stable tension that keeps the network up and running.

Rules of the Game

The people who build cryptoeconomic systems (public blockchain developers) go about their days with a series of about how these networks should work. Most of these assumptions are predicated on real-life experience with other cryptonetwork protocols, past and present. These assumptions are as follows:

> *Beware of centralization*: Any two individuals who each hold close to 25 percent of either network mining hashpower or the cryptocurrency itself are dangerously close to being able to induce a hostile fork and destroy network integrity.

> *Most people are rational*: However, some quota of every network will consist of users who behave in ways that are difficult to reason about. Some of these people may attempt to bring down the network, either on purpose or by some incredible accident.

> *Large networks have people who churn in and out*: This creates ebbs and flows in network traffic and usership, but some users will stick and maintain high levels of activity.

> *Censorship is not possible*: Contracts can trust they are receiving complete messages from other contracts.

> *Nodes can talk freely*: Any two nodes can pass messages quickly and easily.

> *Debt and negative reputation claims are unenforceable*: Because anyone using a public chain can create a new wallet address at any time, some kinds of communities can exist only on private chains with limited-issue wallet addresses controlled by a software contract or central authority.

Although many of these assumptions apply to Bitcoin, it doesn't fully exploit them in the service of all the various problems humanity faces today. Its unwieldiness in the creation of long-term debt instruments such as bonds or mortgages is just one example of a major area of human activity—debt financing—that Bitcoin seems ill-suited for.

This is not a knock on Bitcoin, but rather an admission of its forte as a global liquid payments layer. It is not a storage medium, or a useful commodity, or a visible sign of wealth. Expressions of monetary value are numerous in human culture, and the discovery of new ones is, in part, what drives the current flurry of activity around cryptoeconomics.

Why Is Cryptoeconomics Useful?

First and foremost, applied cryptoeconomics is about engineering a layer of defense between public networks and attackers of all sizes. It combines game theoretical system design, encryption, and cryptographic hashing to protect a commonly used, commonly operated resource—in this case, a global transaction state machine.

Because public chains are public, they need to be resilient against attackers with large amounts of computing power. Hence, networks with more nodes, and more geographically distributed nodes, owned by discrete unlinked owners, are considered more secure.

Mining pools contribute to centralization, which is why any pool with larger than 25 percent hashpower is approaching the threshold of network threat. Should two such pools emerge, they might quickly get control of a network.

By using the custom, ASIC-resistant Ethash algorithm and designing the network to quickly increase in difficulty, the protocol designers ensured there would be little incentive for miners to professionalize and consolidate.

Understanding Hashing vs. Encryption

Recall from Chapter 1 that a blockchain consists of three constituent technologies working in combination. They are as follows:

> Cryptographic hashing

> Asymmetric public-key cryptography

> Distributed P2P computing

In the previous chapter, you learned that each block header contains the root hash of the entire chain, along with a hash of the transactions in the block. These two bits of data in the block header are used to create an encryption seed, which in turn generates the DAG file, which expands to 1 GB and serves as a kind of pop-up ingredient tray for the proof-of-work algorithm, which hashes together chunks of data from the DAG in order to look for a winning nonce value that will validate the block.

■ **Note** Large corporations benefit from public chains, too, because they can offset the large cost of a secure, private application data layer. At the launch of the Ethereum Enterprise Alliance on February 28, 2017 in Brooklyn, New York, Ethereum co-founder Joe Lubin noted that, for large organizations, "it doesn't make sense to build on a blockchain that doesn't have a public component, because the cryptoeconomics of going from private to public are pretty much impossible."

Both processes are algorithmic: some information goes in, and different information comes out. But they're used toward different ends.

Encryption

We've talked about encryption already in this book, but let's review: Both Ethereum and Bitcoin accounts use a pair of cryptographic keys, one public and one private, to encrypt transactions sent to their respective virtual machines. (Both networks use the same algorithm called *secp256k1 curve* to perform encryption.) Recall that this is known as public-key encryption, also known as *asymmetric encryption*. This is in contrast to *symmetric encryption,* in which both parties share a public and private key, much the way you and a spouse might share an address and have duplicate house keys.

The symmetric encryption pattern is the one used by most servers today. When servers communicate, they often use the same private key to authenticate each other. This is safe only if you trust the server on the other end of the transaction to keep this private key, which is presumably of mutual value to both parties, secret from any saboteur.

Encryption turns a human-readable string of letters or numbers into an unreadable blob of random letters and numbers with one important caveat. The ciphertext that comes out of encryption algorithms *does not have a fixed length.*

Pretty Good Privacy (PGP) and Advanced Encryption Standard (AES) are popular algorithms for doing this. The RSA encryption algorithm is another widely-used standard in IT departments around the world. However, sometimes public keys generated by these popular encryption algorithms can be very long and unwieldy. Ethereum uses the same *elliptic-curve-based encryption* protocol as Bitcoin, also known as an ECDSA algorithm, which has the advantage of both security and brevity: ECDSA allows for a smaller key size, which reduces storage needs and transmission requirements. However, Vitalik Buterin has said the protocol will likely move away from the current implementation of ECDSA in the future, towards something offering even greater security.

Weaknesses of Encryption

However, encryption also has weaknesses. For one, it has a reputation for being CPU-intensive. For another, private keys may be cryptographically secure, but they aren't impervious to human folly. Private keys must be carefully managed. In fact, the National Institute of Standards and Technology (NIST) provides guidelines for the life cycle of cryptographic keys, based on the sensitivity of the data or keys to be protected, and how much data (or how many key pairs) are being protected.[2]

It should be noted that, if you don't want anyone to decode your message, encryption is not your best choice. The existence of a private key is practically begging for your information to someday be unlocked, presumably by you, but also by anyone who gets ahold of it!

Hashing

Hashing is more secure than encryption, at least in the sense that there exists no private key that can "reverse" a hash back into its original, readable form. Thus, if a machine doesn't need to know the contents of a dataset, it should be given the hash of the dataset instead.

Hashing algorithms take in data just like encryption algorithms, but they produce a string or number of fixed length. Changing just one character in a large dataset will cause the hash to come out completely different. It's basically impossible to put hashed data back into its original form. Popular hashing algorithms include MD5, SHA-1, and SHA-2. Ethereum and Bitcoin protocols both use SHA-256, the strongest hashing algorithm out there.

---

[2]NIST, "Recommendations for key management," https://www.nist.gov/node/563271, 2012.

What Hashes Are Good For

If you recognize the names of those hashing algorithms that start with *SHA*, it's probably because you've seen them in your smartphone or computer's network interface when connecting to Wi-Fi and entering a password. Because hashes are one-way by nature, they're great for comparing two secret values without revealing what they are. Thus, if your computer hashes the Wi-Fi password and hands it to the Wi-Fi router—which knows the password—it should hash the password itself and get the same result. This confirms that you have the right password and are allowed to connect. The advantage here is that anyone snooping on the network never sees the password, only the hash.

Why the Speed of Blocks Matters

Chapter 6 defined a block as a period of time: 15 seconds, to be exact. Many of the subroutines in the mining process are engineered to maintain that block time. However, we haven't stopped to ask whether that block time is "better" than Bitcoin's 10-minute blocks, or whether it is merely characteristic of the way the Ethereum protocol works.

One fact you should know is the latency for Bitcoin nodes around the world. About 95 percent of them can be reached in 12.6 seconds, as measured by an academic team in 2013.[3] This number is proportional to block size, so in a "faster" block time currency, you could have a more responsive network.

However, fast blocks are less secure in the near term, for reasons that we won't get into here. But in their favor, they produce fast confirmation times; in order words, they benefit from more granularity of information. Thus, while nodes may be easier to fool initially, they are drawn powerfully toward the "true" chain within a few generations. The idea that faster blocks are proportionally less secure than slower blocks is false.

To read more about how the speed of block times affects various network characteristics, read this post on the Ethereum blog: https://blog.ethereum.org/2015/09/14/on-slow-and-fast-block-times/.

Ether Issuance Scheme

Ether is created by the network to pay miners. However, some ether was presold in mid-2014 to bootstrap the funding of the network. Approximately 60 million ETH were sold at prices varying from 1,000 to 2,000 ETH per bitcoin. (About 10 percent was allocated to the Ethereum Foundation, and another 10 percent was maintained as a reserve at the time of the presale.)

From the presale forward, the system will issue 15.6 million ether per year in the form of rewards paid to miners. Ether never stops being issued, but the amount issued per year is a smaller and smaller percentage of the overall pool. As you can see in Figure 7-1, the small uptick in the curved line at 2014–2015 indicates the presale period.

---

[3]Swiss Federal Institute of Technology, Zurich, "Information Propagation in the Bitcoin Network," www.tik.ee.ethz.ch/file/49318d3f56c1d525aabf7fda78b23fc0/P2P2013_041.pdf, 2013.

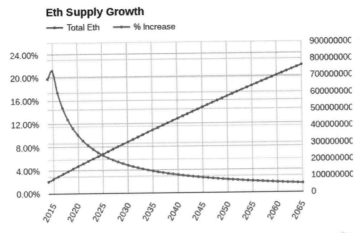

Figure 7-1. *Ether's supply is inflationary, but that isn't necessarily reflected in the price*

Thus, ether's issuance scheme is inflationary (in terms of quantity, not price) until approximately 2025, and deflationary in quantity thereafter. The price of ether is whatever the market dictates, and is predicated mostly on demand of time on the EVM. Like gasoline, the price fluctuations have more to do with how much people are driving—or who's manipulating the price through trading!

Common Attack Scenarios

Next, we'll briefly discuss how the Ethereum protocol addresses some of the most common attack vectors in a P2P network. As covered in Chapter 3 in our exploration of the EVM, the state transition function is bounded to a limited number of computational steps per block. If execution runs longer, it is cut off, and those state changes are reverted. However, fees are still paid to the miners for these rolled-back changes.

The rationale for this design decision in the protocol becomes apparent when viewed through a cryptoeconomic lens. The Ethereum White Paper uses the following examples to demonstrate the usefulness of its specification when the network is under attack:

- If an attacker sends a miner a contract containing an infinite loop, it will eventually run out of gas. However, the transaction is still valid in the sense that the miner can claim a fee from the attacker for each computational step the program took.

- Even if an attacker tries to pay the appropriate gas fee to keep the miner working, the miner will see that the STARTGAS value is excessively high and will know ahead of time that the computation will take too many steps.

145

- Imagine that an attacker is careful with his gas payment: the attacker sends contract code with just enough to make a withdrawal, but not enough to make the balance of the account go down. This is similar to a double-spend attack, in that it creates money out of thin air. However, in Ethereum, this transaction would be entirely rolled back because it ran out of gas in the middle.

Social Proof Between Machines

It's weird to think of machines as being social, but a network of machines is just that: always talking. Proof of work is kind of like social proof among human beings. *Social proof* is a form of conformity, in which one individual—unsure about how to behave—emulates the behavior of those who seem to know better. In many cases, this means emulating a majority.

How can this phenomenon possibly secure a network? Well, in the Ethereum and Bitcoin networks, the order of transactions that is benighted as "true" is *simply the order that a majority of nodes say is true.* It's no more factual than that. This is why the 51 percent attack is a real phenomenon: it's an enormous carrot for anyone to spin up a plurality of miners and fork the network to begin siphoning value. It's nothing more than the enormous cost—the sheer stupid unprofitability—of such an attack that stops it from happening. It's expensive to buy, lease, or operate thousands of gigahashes of computing power.

Security as the Network Scales

Today the market cap of ether is small, but if only a fraction of global web services shift to utilize it, the value of ether could grow in excess of its natural price deflation. However, the price of ether doesn't matter much if you're thinking of it as a commodity: that is, fuel for paying application hosting costs on the EVM.

As the price increases and decreases, it attracts speculators and market makers, who drive volatility even higher in times of excessive trading volume. This in turn changes the profit margin for miners, who may choose to turn off their nodes until ether is at a price where they are again getting a net profit.

Volatility creates the possibility for malicious node operators and financial market-makers to collude, driving down the price to reduce network hashpower, and then flipping on an entire farm of miners intended to fork the chain into a new state—while performing a double-spend in the process. As of this writing, such collusion hasn't succeeded, and it may never. Already many prominent Wall Street banks have announced Ethereum development programs to be run internally or in cooperation with outside consultants, so the network's robustness is under less doubt every passing day

More About Cryptoeconomics

The title of this section comes from a Reddit post by Vitalik Buterin in which he lays out four more attack scenarios, with some thoughts about how they might transpire. You can find those at `www.reddit.com/r/ethereum/comments/453sid/empirical_cryptoeconomics/`.

If you're interested in the cultural impact of cryptoeconomic activity, try this essay by CoMakery founder Noah Thorp: `https://medium.com/@noahthorp/how-society-will-be-transformed-by-crypto-economics-b02b6765ca8c#.e10qayhio`.

Summary

The briefness of this chapter is one indication of the novelty of this subgenre of economics. Though new, it will inevitably be complex, as each cryptocurrency comes with its own issuance parameters.

For some guidance on the future, it might be useful to look to none other than the Federal Reserve for how these questions might mete out over the decades. David Andolfatto of the St. Louis Fed wrote in a blog post in early 2015 that the US central bank might have reason to consider a national cryptocurrency. He described it as follows:

> *Imagine that the Fed, as the core developer, makes available an open source Bitcoin-like protocol (suitably modified) called Fedcoin. The key point is this: the Fed is in the unique position to credibly fix the exchange rate between Fedcoin and the USD (the exchange rate could be anything, but let's assume par). What justifies my claim that the Fed has a comparative advantage over some private enterprise that issues (say) BTC backed by USD at a fixed exchange rate? The problem with such an enterprise is precisely the problem faced by countries that try to peg their currency unilaterally to some other currency. Unilateral fixed exchange rate systems are inherently unstable because the agency fixing the BTC/USD exchange rate cannot credibly commit not to run out of USD reserves to meet redemption waves of all possible sizes. In fact, the structure invites a speculative attack.[4]*

In a talk given in Frankfurt earlier that year where he first aired these proposals, he referred to the system as *Fedwire for all*. With any luck, you'll recall our discussion of the Fedwire system from Chapter 3 and our discussion of the EVM.

Next, we'll get back to the command line and learn how dapps are deployed.

---

[4]MacroMania, "FedCoin: The Desirability of a Government Cryptocurrency," `http://andolfatto.blogspot.co.uk/2015/02/fedcoin-on-desirability-of-government.html`, 2015.

CHAPTER 8

Dapp Deployment

As you'll see, deploying dapps is an adventure in the frontier of a new computing paradigm

A *distributed application,* or *dapp,* shares some of the same ideals as the rest of the EVM protocol: the promise immutability. Dapps are composed of smart contracts that, as noted many times in this book, are executed by all nodes on the Ethereum network at approximately the same time.

Dapps in practice are like universally available web services running on the EVM, but made accessible to users via a normal HTML/CSS/JavaScript front end that they can access through their web browser or a smartphone application, or an Ethereum browser such as Mist.

Note   This chapter tackles topics aimed at developers with preexisting skills. If you're a new coder, read this chapter thoroughly along with Chapter 9. Then, pick up a JavaScript beginner book to improve your scripting skills. Next, visit `http://solidity.eth.guide` for more Solidity language tutorials.

Running blockchain-based application clients is far easier than managing clients in a cloud-hosted paradigm. Hub-and-spoke web applications scale vertically, reflecting the individual servers they run on. In contrast, an Ethereum application scales horizontally— the *way you'd want* a cloud application to scale.

Although it's true that today cryptonetworks are significantly constrained in terms of transaction processing power, they will get faster as other components of the protocol mature.

© Chris Dannen 2017
C. Dannen, *Introducing Ethereum and Solidity*, DOI 10.1007/978-1-4842-2535-6_8

Seven Ways to Think About Smart Contracts

Behind every dapp is a series of smart contracts. Smart contracts are useful in these scenarios, which may make fun problem areas for prototyping:

> Maintain an accounting system for something in the real world, or for other contracts

> Create forwarding contracts, such as a savings account that resends income to a separate bucket automatically

> Manage a relationship between several parties, such as a freelancer agreement or payroll

> Act as a software library for other contracts

> Act as controllers for other systems or sets of contracts

> Serve as application-specific logic for a communal web service

> Serve as a utility that developers can use on a single-serving basis, such as a random number generator

Dapp development brings with it all sorts of new concerns for application developers, as well as an understanding of the Web3 JavaScript API and the Solidity programming language. Hopefully, you feel prepared to work with these tools directly after reading most of this book!

To get a better idea of the kinds of dapps being built today, check out http://dapps.ethercasts.com, operated by EtherCasts.

Dapp Contract Data Models

The first thing you'll need to know to deploy a working contract is what kind of data you can store in the EVM, and where you're storing it.

As we discussed in prior chapters, every contract address in the Ethereum network has storage space for its smart contracts. This storage space has no limit, except what you're willing to pay. As of this writing, storage space costs about $0.018 per kilobyte.

The Solidity language makes it easy to use contracts as little relational databases. To make this easier, the Solidity language has two familiar data types we haven't mentioned yet:

> Mappings

> Structs

To learn more about using these types in Solidity, consult http://solidity.eth.guide. At its most basic, a contract's individual storage space is a key/value store with 2^{256} possible keys and the same number of values. That's enough space for pretty much any kind of database structure you feel like creating.

▓ **Note**   Recall that object attributes are sometimes referred to by developers as *keys*, as in the phrase *key/value pair* or *key/value store*. In our human example, a key/value pair might be footSize = 11. A table containing everyone's foot size on a dedicated server is an example of a key/value store. As a stateful transaction machine, you can think of the entire EVM as a giant key/value store that shows account balances.

Hopefully by now, you are already picturing the kinds of simple data structures you could create and use in Solidity contracts. In the next section, we'll begin breaking down distributed app architecture.

How an EVM Back End Talks to a JS Front End

The gap between the Ethereum network and what might be called the *HTTP network*, otherwise known as the Web, can indeed be traversed. Let's say a customer enters a lunch order on a dapp-powered web site from a conventional web browser. In order to successfully pass data about her order (how many milkshakes?) between her browser and the EVM, the dapp's front end must "send" the data to the EVM in a certain format.

▓ **Note**   Dapps may not require their own set of contracts; instead, they may be able to call certain public functions in other contracts to make use of their functionality. For every function declared public in a smart contract, Solidity automatically creates an accessor function so that other contracts can call it.

In computing, *data-interchange formats* work much like the international postal service. Although different servers around the world may be running different operating systems, written in different languages, by totally different minds, they must at some point exchange data with a server that is not like them.

To get the "translation" correct, programmers engineer their programs to send information to other programs in a certain *notations*. Usually, the notation describes a format for an entire object (defined in Chapter 1 as a set of attributes and values). For example, a human data object might include height, weight, eye color, foot size, and so on.

JSON-RPC

In today's web applications, JavaScript code can pass information across the Web by using a common object notation called *JavaScript Object Notation* (*JSON*). JSON objects can contain numbers, strings, and ordered sequences of values for certain attributes.

There are two important data objects in Web3.js, which are roughly equivalent to JSON in the way they are passed between the front and back ends of an Ethereum-powered application. They are called *JSON-RPC objects* and they come with the Web3.js library. Installation of Web3.js is covered below. These two objects are used in the following ways:

- web3.eth is used specifically for blockchain interactions.

- web3.shh is used specifically for Whisper interactions.

Whisper is a private messaging protocol that is itself a part of the larger Ethereum protocol. You'll learn more about Whisper and its place on the roadmap in Chapter 11.

In motion, you can think of JSON-RPC objects as passing back and forth constantly between the front end (on the HTTP Web) and the back end (the Ethereum Web).

Web 3 Is Here (Almost)

The JavaScript library called Web3.js is part of the new *Web 3 specification*. You can find the GitHub page for the Web 3 project at https://github.com/ethereum/web3.js/.

Web 3 is a general term for the decentralized web, just as Web 2 was defined by web-hosted applications and services. Web 1 refers to the original World Wide Web, which hosted static pages. Ever since, the Hypertext Transfer Protocol has been evolving to add more methods and to support ever more sophisticated content and scripts.

Web 3 is very much a vision that centers on the Ethereum protocol in particular. It is generally considered to have three components:

Peer-to-peer identity and messaging system

Shared state (a blockchain)

Decentralized file storage

The first two check boxes are complete: the Ethereum network is up and running, and transactions work! The third leg on the stool, decentralized file storage, is part of the Swarm project, which you'll learn more about in Chapter 11.

In the Web 3 paradigm, there are no web servers. There are no caches, reverse proxies, load balancers, content delivery networks (CDNs), or other vestiges of legacy large-scale web application deployment. Even decentralized domain name servers (DNS) will be free. When Swarm storage comes online, it will be cheap, just like Ethereum's web-hosting component.

For developers and hackers of all types, Web 3 blows up the "freemium" application deployment model, in which more and more users and scale bring you higher and higher hosting bills. In the EVM, you can control your costs by writing efficient code, and you can count on anyone on Earth being able to access your application from day one.

Let's zoom back into the specifics of dapp development and see how the Web we know today talks to the EVM.

Experimenting with the JavaScript API

In Chapter 6, you saw how easy it is to interact with the EVM by typing commands into the JavaScript console in Geth. When you're doing this, you're really just calling individual JavaScript methods that come with the Ethereum JavaScript API. These JavaScript methods you type into the Geth console are being interpreted by a JIT-like JavaScript interpreter that is unique to Geth. This is called *interactive* use of the JSRE, or using it in *interactive mode*.

However, the Ethereum JavaScript API methods can also be exposed to normal web applications, allowing them to talk to the EVM.

Using Geth for Dapp Deployment

Although other Ethereum clients are popular, Geth (which is written in the Go language developed at Google) and its easy-breezy interpretations of JavaScript make it the quickest way to connect a front-end web application on the traditional HTTP Web with a back-end EVM contract.

Because these are JavaScript methods being interpreted by Geth into EVM code, it's possible to string them together into scripts, which of course is the natural use for JavaScript in the first place. This is referred to as using it *noninteractively*.

▓ **Note** Noninteractive use of the JavaScript API is the whole reason for what we call *computer programming*. This is, generally speaking, the goal of programming, or writing a program: to automate what would be otherwise manual commands typed into the terminal, like the ones you typed to install Geth. When performing complex computations or building analytical models, these strings of instructions can get long and tiresome.

By writing strings of instructions in a plain-text file, the programmer can make a program condensed, quick, efficient, and repeatable.

Another goal of programming is to separate the tasks a human operator would be entering, and do them concurrently in *threads*, so the whole job takes less time. As you saw with Geth when it first started up, you couldn't do anything with that command-line window while it was synchronizing, and indeed that thread would not stop as long as Geth was running.

By building a console on top of Geth, the Ethcore developers have allowed you, the operator of the console, to issue commands while Geth is synchronizing in the background, in another thread on your local machine.

Next, you'll learn about ideal web development frameworks for connecting to the EVM as a back end.

Using Meteor with the EVM

If you're a JavaScript developer, you may have heard about Meteor.js, a library that lets you write reactive web applications that run symmetrical code on the server and client.

This full-stack framework is excellent for real-time web applications, but is useful for Ethereum front-end development because it is so well suited to writing *single-page applications*, or *SPAs*.

Here's why so many Ethereum developers love Meteor:

> It's written entirely in JavaScript, as are the tools.

> You get a whole developer environment out of the box.

> Deployment is super easy.

> Interfaces are fully reactive (similar to Angular.js).

> Uses a NoSQL data model called MiniMongo, which can be autopersisted to local smart-contract storage.

To learn more about building Ethereum apps with Meteor.js, check out https:// github.com/ethereum/wiki/wiki/Dapp-using-Meteor.

This URL is also listed on tutorials.eth.guide. Next you'll learn about installing the Web3.js library onto your development machine so you can begin messing around with contracts locally.

Install Web3.js to Build an Ethereum-Enabled Web Application

The Web3.js library communicates through RPC to a local node. The library works with any Ethereum node, as long as it is exposing its RPC layer. You'll need to install this library on your local machine to do development, and on your web server to run your front-end application.

This is exposed by default on private chains, even if you do not start your chain in Geth with this command flagged.

In effect, you can think of your Ethereum node as the bare-metal layer, exposing the EVM through its RPC layer. That RPC layer can send and receive web3.eth and web3.shh objects with a web server that is also running Web3.js.

To install Web3.js in your local development environment, open the Terminal and use the installation library that you're most comfortable with:

- *npm*: npm install web3
- *bower*: bower install web3
- *meteor*: meteor add ethereum:web3
- *vanilla*: link the dist./web3.min.js

Then you need to create a Web3 instance and set your localhost as a provider. To continue learning how to work with Web3.js, go to http://dapps.eth.guide.

Next, you'll see how to execute JavaScript files in the Geth console.

Executing Contracts in the Console

A full tutorial in dapp deployment would take many pages and could be performed dozens of possible ways. This section instead focuses on getting started quickly.

You can upload your smart contract files directly in Geth, sending them in a transaction to the EVM by simply adding the --exec argument and then writing JavaScript code pointing to a local script. For example:

```
$ geth --exec 'loadScript("/Desktop/test.js")'
```

In fact, you can even execute JavaScript that is sitting on another machine, as long as it is running Geth:

```
$ geth --exec 'loadScript("/Desktop/test.js")' attach
https://100.100.100.100:8000
```

The next section covers the architecture of Ethereum-enabled applications, and how they diverge from traditional web architecture.

How Contracts Expose an Interface

When using the JavaScript dapp API, calling a contract via an abstraction layer such as the eth.contract() function will send back an object with all the functions that contract can run when called in JavaScript.

To standardize this introspective functionality, the Ethereum protocol comes with something called the *application binary interface*, otherwise known as the *Contract ABI*. The ABI behaves like an API, creating a standard syntax for contracts to be called by applications.

The ABI dictates that the contract will send back an array that delineates the proper call signature and the available contract functions.

It may be surprising to some developers, especially those hailing from the Apple developer environment, that there are no frameworks that "come with" Ethereum to enable the easy writing of common application components.

Although the Ethereum protocol may be generally featureless, there's still a need to make contracts interact in predictable ways in common use cases. These scenarios include currency units, name registry, and trading on exchanges. The ABI is a concession to such scenarios.

ABI contains the word *binary* because in the EVM, the level below the application layer is the one that runs EVM bytecode.

You can find this specification at https://github.com/ethereum/wiki/wiki/ Ethereum-Contract-ABI#functions or at http://abi.eth.guide.

Standards for smart contracts usually consist of sets of function signatures for a few common methods, such as sending, receiving, registering, deleting, and so on.

Recommendations for Prototyping

The first thing to know about prototyping Solidity contracts is that you do not necessarily need an Ethereum node to test your contracts. You can use the Ethereum VM Contract Simulator, `https://github.com/EtherCasts/evm-sim/`. This simulator allows developers to test their contracts in isolation when they don't have access to the testnet; for example, when working from a netbook.

Here are other best practices for prototyping, when you get to the stage where you are testing with live ether:

> Don't use too much ether per contract, and when possible, program upper limits on how much contracts will hold. This is a good fail-safe in the event that a bug traps your funds. Simply don't use too much when testing with live ether.

> Keep your contracts modular and easy to understand. Whenever possible, abstract out functionality into libraries that can be individually tested. Limit the number of variables and length of your functions. Document everything.

> Use the Checks-Effects-Interactions pattern. This means you shouldn't write programs that wait for return data from another contract before proceeding; this will cause time-outs. Generally speaking, you can avoid this by performing checks on the data you get back before changing state.

> Write your own intermediaries. Because the EVM is such an unforgiving platform, it's incumbent on you to create mechanisms for your own programs that act as fail-safes.

> As mentioned in Chapter 5, in the token contract tutorial, developers are converging around standards for some types of contracts. You can register your contracts with a third-party service such as Etherchain so that other people can use them. You'll see publicly listed contracts at `https://etherchain.org/contracts`.

> Test, test, test! You'll find testing resources at `http://test.eth.guide`.

You've looked at several contracts that were clearly written for demonstration purposes. What kind of simple smart contracts might you create in the service of real dapps, and what is the best way to deploy them? That's the subject of the last section of this chapter.

Third-Party Deployment Libraries

Deploying more-sophisticated smart contracts and connecting them to the Web is slightly beyond the scope of this book—in part because it is an area of rapid development and constant changes. It's also fairly difficult, and requires some patience, as of this writing.

As a result, developer tools are a major area of active development in the Ethereum community.

Leading groups of developers have created tools to make contract and dapp deployment easier to achieve. Here are some of the projects you should be aware of:

- Monax tutorials and Solidity contracts

- OpenZeppelin smart contracts

- Truffle deployment, testing, and asset creation environment

- Dapple, a developer environment for complex contract systems

- Populus, contract development framework written in Python

- Embark, dapp development framework written in JavaScript

- Ether Pudding, a package builder

- Solium, a linter for Solidity

There are many more dapp guides, tutorials, best practices, and sample projects than this book can cover. You will find up-to-date links for all of these tools and libraries, plus a lot more, at `http://dapp.eth.guide`.

In addition, a collection of Gitter channels where you can find help with development and deployment can be found at `http://help.eth.guide`.

Summary

In this chapter, you learned about the kinds of contracts Ethereum is useful for writing and how to go about deploying them. Also covered were the ways that smart contracts can communicate with an application's front end.

Ethereum dapp development isn't easy, but it's becoming more and more approachable every day. Join the Gitter channels or join a local developer community. As of this writing, 81,424 members and 2,257 interested people are in 450 Ethereum Meetups all over the world—in 218 cities and 57 countries to be exact. To find one near you, search Meetup (`www.meetup.com`).

In the next chapter, you'll deploy your own private blockchain to get a better understanding of how chains work.

CHAPTER 9

■ ■ ■

Creating Private Chains

Contrary to what public-chain enthusiasts argue, private chains do have merit as learning tools, and may ultimately have uses for large corporations, nation-states, or nongovernmental organizations (NGOs). However, it should be said that blockchains are not inherently better for all databases and networks

In the last few chapters, we've focused on deploying smart contracts, dapps, and tokens. In this chapter, we'll engage in a brief discussion of blockchains as databases to more thoroughly understand how the chains themselves are deployed.

Private and Permissioned Chains

A *private chain* is just a cloud database achieved by way of the peer-to-peer Ethereum protocol: it's a silo that you control and that you can grant access to.

This should be contrasted with a *permissioned blockchain*, which like an enterprise software application has defined roles with permissions that can be set by a central administrator.

Big picture, private chains are in no way inherently better than cloud databases. In practice, the utility of the Ethereum protocol comes from bringing disparate groups together to share secure infrastructure, instead of duplicating effort. Today, the Ethereum network is fully operational, however it has not scaled to the point where existing web application providers could migrate. But this is after only two years of development, and as you'll see in Chapter 11, the future milestones are fairly incredible and coming to pass on schedule.

By contrast, the HTTP Web has been under development since 1989.[1] Decentralized cloud storage, namespaces, and other common elements of the HTTP Web have yet to be reproduced in the Ethereum Web, but will be soon. Let's move on so you can create your very own custom blockchain, to get a better understanding of how they work.

---

[1]Wikipedia, "Hypertext Transfer Protocol," https://en.wikipedia.org/wiki/Hypertext_ Transfer_Protocol, 2016.

© Chris Dannen 2017
C. Dannen, *Introducing Ethereum and Solidity*, DOI 10.1007/978-1-4842-2535-6_9

Setting Up a Local Private Chain

A private chain is of limited usefulness because, as established in Chapters 6 and 7, the security of a chain is proportional to the number of nodes that are mining on it. When you start up your chain, it will have only one miner: you.

However, starting up a local private chain is a nice way to create a testnet in a classroom environment, enabling students to mine and thus execute their and their classmates' transactions and smart contracts. Once you see how easy it is, you will appreciate the highly generalized nature of the EVM.

The content is the same as the genesis field provided by the config parameter:

Because you already have Geth installed, and you know how to use the command line, you need only three things to create a private chain:

Custom genesis JSON file

Custom network ID (a number)

A directory where the network ID file is stored

You can make up the network ID; it simply can't be numerals 1 or 2, which are already taken by the testnet (2) and the main network (1). We'll go over the custom genesis file next.

CREATING YOUR BLOCKCHAIN GENESIS FILE

Every blockchain has to start somewhere, and in this, your very own Garden of Eden, you get to plant the seed that becomes a private chain. Block 0 does not point to a predecessor block, and is thus unlike any other block in the chain. The protocol ensures that your chain will accept only blocks that can trace their roots back to this genesis block by looking at the root hash in the block header.

Here's how you create the custom genesis file.

First, open your text editor. You're going to create a network called 765, so you'll set 765 as the nonce value. It needs to be a nonzero number. You can find the code at https://github.com/chrisdannen/Introducing-Ethereum-and-Solidity/blob/master/genesis765.json or under the Chapter 9 heading at http://eth.guide.

In your text editor, paste in the following text:

```
{
"nonce": "0x0000000000000765",
"timestamp": "0x0",
"parentHash": "0x0000000000000000000000000000000000000000000000000000000000000000",
"extraData": "0x0",
```

```
"gasLimit": "0x4c4b40",
"difficulty": "0x400",
"mixhash": "0x0000000000000000000000000000000000000000000000000000
000000000",
"coinbase": "0x0000000000000000000000000000000000000000",
"alloc": {
}
```

Save this file to your desktop and call it **genesis765.json**.

To open your new chain with a JavaScript console, like the one you used in Chapter 6, open the Terminal and then type the following seven elements on one line:

- geth

- console

- --networkid

- --genesis

- The path to the Genesis file

- --datadir

- A data directory to store your new chain

You will create a hidden directory called ~/.ethereum/chain765 to store your chain. Your complete Terminal command should look like this:

```
geth console --networkid 765 --genesis ~/Desktop/genesis765.json
--datadir ~/.ethereum/chain765
```

■ **Note**   Type eth at the console of your new chain to see a list of available JavaScript methods. In a group testing environment, you can use commands such as net.peercount to see how many other people are mining on your chain, and other miscellany.

And that's it! Your new chain is up and running, and you can use the console just as you did in Chapter 6. Remember that you need to turn on your miner with the miner.start() command in the console before your contracts will execute on this testnet.

Optional Flags to Use with New Chains

You can use other flags when creating a new chain to customize your testnet environment:

--nodiscover: This prevents anyone with the same genesis file and the same network ID from connecting to your chain accidentally.

--maxpeers 0: If you know how many peers you want connected to your node (say you have a classroom with a limited number of students), you can delimit your chain's number of participants with this flag.

--rpcapi "db,eth,net,web3": Enables RPC and various Web3.js APIs that are accessed over RPC.

--rpcport "8080": The default port for Geth is 8080, but you can choose a different one with this flag.

--rpccorsdomain "http://eth.guide/": Use this flag to specify the domains of servers that are allowed to connect to your node and make RPC calls.

--identity "TestnetMainNode": This gives your chain a human-readable name, which makes it easily identifiable when in a list of peers.

Private Blockchains in Production Usage

In this chapter we've presented the concept of private blockchains as a sandbox for learning Solidity and the Ethereum smart contract deployment paradigm. However, some people are quite serious about taking private blockchains out of the testnet role and using them in an enterprise or small-to-medium business computing context, to create real web services.

This is antithetical to the security model that the Ethereum developers had in mind when they designed the protocol. In practice, your private chain presents little incentive for hackers to compromise it. After all, the value of the tokens mined on your chain (or any chain, for that matter) is only what other people will pay for them.

Stop and think about that for a moment! The main network, the network we consider the Ethereum public blockchain, is no different than any other chain. Testnets and the main network are technically indistinguishable, except for the rate of participation they get, and the fact that one is socially accepted as the main public chain. If you're surprised, then you've forgotten the core mantra of Ethereum: generalize everything, and keep the protocol featureless.

What makes the main network *main* is the fact that it was started (and later forked) by Vitalik Buterin and the rest of the Ethereum Core development team. It is only the trust, interest, and curiosity in those individuals that keeps people using the main chain.

There is no technical feature inside Mist or Geth that could not be changed with a protocol fork, which would designate a new chain as the main one. (In fact, this happened after the DAO hack incident in summer of 2016, leaving behind an "old" chain called Ethereum Classic, which is still being mined today by some miners.)

This is the inherent flexibility—and impermanence—that makes the network resilient. This kind of agility is necessary now, in the early days of the network, but will become less and less appealing as the network grows and users seek more predictability and reliability. Before long, state forks will be almost impossible to pull off owing to the sheer size of the network, and the likelihood of another Ethereum chain popping up becomes less and less.

Indeed, Ethereum has much maturation to endure before it is running large, mission-critical business logic contracts. However, when you consider the incredible ease of use, it's easy to see why Ethereum, and networks like it, are bound to replace the stiff and aging Hypertext Transfer Protocol.

Summary

With all the ease and guarantees of private and permissioned blockchains, why have a public chain at all? Why don't large corporations merely spin up large networks of nodes in their worldwide offices, creating their own private Ethereum networks?

The short answer is that it's easier and cheaper for large organizations to build on top of distributed infrastructure which they don't have to pay to build and maintain. Even better, they don't have to pay to secure it; the network itself grows more secure as organizations add their nodes.

Indeed, only a public chain is truly trustworthy for high-value transactions, because only a public chain is secured by so much proof of work. For all its users know, a private or permissioned EVM instance has been altered in ways that make it unfair or untrustworthy. With the public chain, protocol forks would need to be initiated by all miners to become effective network-wide.

In the next chapter, we'll discuss what individuals and companies might choose to build on the public chain.

CHAPTER 10

Use Cases

Proof of work, decentralization, Merkle and Patricia trees, asymmetric cryptography, smart contracts ... What can you make with such ingredients?

Whether Ethereum is useful, and indeed groundbreaking, is best evaluated in the same terms as other network protocols. It's been so long since Ted Nelson coined the term *hypertext* in 1965, with his Xanadu project, that it's easy to forget why people liked HTTP and its sibling, HTML. It had exactly one method, GET, which would request a page from a web server. The only acceptable response was an HTML page.[1]

In many respects, the Ethereum network today is in the same stages as the Hypertext Transfer Protocol and the Hypertext Markup Language back in 1989. Its existence alone is a boon compared to what came before, so much so that the first iteration of the network feels almost like a one-trick pony.

Subsequent iterations will show that its seemingly sparse specification produces immensely sophisticated software. This chapter is dedicated to illustrating the kinds of applications that are on the near horizon.

Chains Everywhere

To many cryptocurrency maximalists, the future will be replete with blockchains, which will have long since replaced every other technological paradigm. This will probably never come to pass—because traditional databases work fine for most things—but new interactions will result from these stateful networks that software developers and designers may not foresee today. And these interactions will encompass not just humans, but also machines working with an unprecedented free will. In the future, you may encounter the Ethereum protocol running below the surface in many of the everyday technological interactions you make. We'll talk about how this future might develop in the following sections.

---

[1]W3.org, "W3 History," www.w3.org/History/19921103-hypertext/hypertext/WWW/Protocols/HTTP.html, 2016.

© Chris Dannen 2017
C. Dannen, *Introducing Ethereum and Solidity*, DOI 10.1007/978-1-4842-2535-6_10

The Internet of Ethereum Things

For large hardware makers, settling on industry standards for Internet of Things (IoT) has been difficult. Ethereum offers a secure, ownerlesss protocol that anyone can use. As a result, it has widely been seen as a boon for IoT. Some examples of IoT interactions on the Ethereum network might include the following:

> *Device-to-device payment policies*: Let's say you want to allow your phone to spend up to $5 without asking your permission. Such an agreement could be presented much as an end-user license agreement (EULA) is for a mobile application today, but today EULAs are not empowered to move money. In a smart contract, the terms of an agreement you might customize, your phone would be able to buy things it knows you need. For example, say you run out of data on your LTE plan; it could pay for extra bandwidth, and even negotiate a price, without interrupting you to "approve" the purchase.

> *Encoding value or financial contracts onto retail objects*: It is difficult to merchandize intellectual property such as music or video, without a physical good to put in a product photo or on a store shelf. The same goes for financial products, which are hard to market because of their abstract nature. Gift-card-like objects in any size and shape could be used to sell financial products and services in a retail setting, by merely printing or encoding a contract address onto the item.

> *Hardware wallets*: You may have seen small computer-like devices being marketed as hardware wallets for bitcoins or ether. Hardware wallets are USB-powered devices that connect to your computer and use its Internet connection to access the blockchain. Like any other node, a hardware wallet creates itself an address, and stores the private key (encrypted, of course) right there on the piece of hardware. Held in a media safe, hardware wallets are revolutionary in wealth management because they allow you to safely keep in your possession an arbitrarily large number of cryptoassets yourself.

▓ **Note**   Hardware wallets are generally safer than storing coins on your smartphone or PC, where you might forget they're there, and accidentally lose them—for example, by formatting your hard drive without first backing up your private key. These devices are also quite durable. More important, they are typically built from audited, open source code and specifications, so you can rest assured your coins are kept safe from malware that might infect a computer or phone.

166

To see options for hardware wallets and other retail Ethereum gear, check out the product listing at http://wallets.eth.guide.

Retail and E-Commerce

The Ethereum and Bitcoin blockchains also promise to change the way we buy normal retail goods.

Peer-to-peer marketplace escrow contracts: Escrow contracts are used in a marketplace in which the buyer and seller do not know, or trust, each other. In an *escrow contract*, both the buyer and seller of a given item put up collateral in the same amount as the purchase. *Collateral* is something of value, held in trust, to secure a transaction in good faith. Only after the buyer confirms that the item has been delivered will the collateral be released back to the buyer and seller. This ensures that if either party tries to cheat the other, they end up sacrificing approximately the same amount they gain by cheating—pretty irrational!

Machine-readable patterns in public spaces: In programming, there is a concept of a *pull request*, whereby one collaborator requests for a project administrator to merge in code he or she has written. You can imagine an invoice to be a pull request for payment. Providing machine-readable codes on clothing or name tags would allow customers in retail spaces to interact with products or services and be invoiced passively, with a guarantee (presumably in a collateralized smart contract form) that the invoices will be resolved.

Community and Government Financing

The way we finance everything from home loans to national debt might radically change as a result of smart contacts. In the US, Ethereum projects might take advantage of the JOBS Act passed in 2012 to relax restrictions on small business funding. The Title III component of this act, known as the CROWDFUND Act, creates a way for companies to use crowdfunding to issue securities, and went into effect May 16, 2016.

Crowdfunding: Because cryptocurrencies are so liquid (fast and easy to send from account to account), they have become a popular choice for denominating donations in crowdfunding campaigns. With the advent of the equity crowdfunding laws in the United States, we may see Ethereum smart contracts being used to create all kinds of incentive, payout, or dividend structures for backers who contribute to a new project. The crowdfunding of the Ethereum project itself, which raised $18 million in bitcoins, pioneered an unheard-of strategy for popularizing and endowing an open source protocol and governing nonprofit foundation. It's easy to imagine how a similar crowdfunding paradigm could be used to finance local public works, such as bridges and parks.

Federal currency issuance: Both central banks and retail banks around the world have expressed interest in the issuance of digital currencies. It's conceivable that a government might beat private currencies to the punch by starting a federally mined chain and issuing a native fiat coin on that network.

Human and Organizational Behavior

People outside large organizations may also benefit from Ethereum in the following domains:

Freelance employment: Ethereum's de facto role as an accounting service makes it ideal for managing teams of far-flung freelancers. Better yet, contracts can be used to form new teams or get two existing groups collaborating, without needing to alter the organizational structure of the business.

Coordinated private transit: Paying strangers for ride sharing, apartment sharing, bike sharing, and other communal services becomes easy and cheap, no matter who is administering the group. There's no need to build an entire reputation system as long as the group members use consistent wallet addresses from week to week or month to month.

■ **Note**   In the first year of the Ethereum network, there was much ado about the concept of a *decentralized autonomous organization*, or DAO. Any Fortune 500 management consultant can tell you that businesses of all sizes are already highly automated. Perhaps someday this automation will all take place with Ethereum, but until then, we'll acknowledge the acronym and move on to more practical discussions.

Customer and employee "pulse" surveys: The concept of a pulse survey is exactly what it sounds like: a regular check-in with a stakeholder you value, to make sure things are going well. Both employees and customers can benefit from regular surveying, but it's challenging. With customers, it's a marketing challenge; it's hard to get space on their smartphone screens without a phone number or a mobile application installed on each user's device. For HR departments, the problem is even more tricky; employees might spend all day in the building and never speak their mind about what's really going on. As an application, Ethereum-enabled wallets are Trojan horses for all kinds of messaging. They could be used for multiple subcurrencies and communities, making them into highly trafficked virtual spaces where people can send and receive information, as well as payments, tokens, and currencies.

Small companies doing big things: In the past, banks, insurance companies, and other institutions attempted to grow as large as possible in an attempt to maximize credibility. When many services—perhaps even government—are provided by the EVM, the threshold for doing business with an unknown entrepreneur naturally drops. Without the risk of them absconding with your cash, why not invest or participate in a crowdfunding event? In a world where fraud and embezzlement are next to impossible, owing to the transparent, predictable, and public nature of public-chain smart contracts, it becomes much easier to offer monetary support to people who need it.

Financial and Insurance Applications

Some of the functions performed by banks will be possible for small businesses to undertake in the Ethereum network.

Everything a bank does, unbundled and delivered as a service in pure software: Unbundled financial services would include complementary currencies, savings accounts, escrow accounts, trusts, wills, and various financial contracts such as swaps, derivatives, and hedging contracts.

Semifinancial applications in which work is being done for money: When proof of an employee's work product can be ascertained by a computer (say, by looking at that employee's sales records in a database), applications might provide provably fair bonus structures with dynamic terms, which exist outside the legacy payroll system. These systems might be referencing employment contracts that are also smart contracts.

Crop insurance: Commodities traders are fond of trading futures and other derivatives that are based on farm crops as the underlying assets. Scientifically observable data such as temperature, barometric pressure, or humidity could be collected by independent sensor motes connected to the Ethereum network, providing accurate endpoints for weather data that might trigger a contract to pay out one way or another.

Community trust: A savings bank written in pure software, whereby one customer can stake another funds, could be trustlessly executed by a smart contract that has the authority to pull collateral, and even loan payments, from an account. Multisignature addresses might ensure appropriate sign-off by human intermediaries in the case of custodial accounts or other special cases.

Inventory and Accounting Systems

Keeping immutable inventory of physical goods, in a supply chain context, may be another area where public chains can shine:

Representing serialized assets such as gold stored in a vault: If you store gold in a bank vault, how do you know it's really there a year later? Because many banks lend out deposits with only a fractional reserve, it's comforting to know your currencies or precious metals are there. Gold, silver, and other instruments inventoried on a blockchain allow owners piece of mind that their wealth won't be lost to a "bail-in" should the bank become insolvent.

Proving the provenance of goods: If a manufactured good has its components inventoried on blockchains by all the original equipment manufacturers, or OEMs, it becomes possible to find out whether a given product is original equipment, or has been altered or repaired.

Token systems that perform simple accounting operations: One easy way of balancing a transaction ledger for a pop-up event (say, for Earth's largest bake sale) would be to create a token which serves as scrip for making purchases at the event. At the door, a smart contract terminal gives every potential customer a certain amount of tokens to spend at the bake sale in exchange for ether. When the event is finished, the sum of the cupcakes you bought will be recorded along with every purchase facilitated by the contract, making it easy for the operators of the bake sale to know if they made a profit.

Software Development

Without a doubt, Ethereum's most disruptive potential lies in its ability to host software and services.

Cloud computing: With data storage coming to the EVM in late 2017, the network will finally begin to resemble a fully fledged web application hosting environment. Distributed consensus protocols make excellent cloud computing platforms because of their *trustless* architecture: there is no need to worry about your complex networking configuration keeping data safe or handling heavy traffic. Such a system may not be suited to every kind of application, but certain easily parallelized software will be.

Long-term application hosting: Some financial contracts are written like time capsules. But how do you ensure that a computer program will still be around to execute in 50 or 100 years? One way is to develop it as a public service; individuals can host documents and be sure the network will still be running, even if they're long gone.

Cheap, resilient, censorship-free public document hosting: Vital documents such as birth certificates, tax returns, court summons, immigration forms, health records, and other unstructured data could easily be encrypted and stored in a blockchain for certain retrieval by third parties. Private organizations today account for most background-check activity and credit reporting. This is problematic to say the least; a public chain might offer a "permanent web" where these documents can be hosted for posterity.

Gaming, Gambling, and Investing

Already, blockchain developers have launched a number of provably fair games of chance, to demonstrate the power of the network. In the future, this sort of application might extend to the following scenarios:

Peer-to-peer gambling: Laws notwithstanding, it's hard to set up geographically extensive gambling networks, because few people trust their bookmaker to hold large amounts of money. Creating bets in pure software—a Main Street way of describing a smart contract—is all too easy in Ethereum. Imagine, for example, a betting contract that simply bets on the value of the nonce, or some other such random event that takes place anyway as the chain maintains consensus.

Prediction markets: Prediction markets attempt to use large-scale betting markets to determine the real-life outcome of events. A government that bases decisions upon prediction markets, in an attempt to automate itself and improve efficacy, is called a *futarchy*.

Stable-value cryptoassets: Cryptocurrencies are notoriously volatile. Because their exchange is not mediated by any third party, there are no chargebacks, making it a perfect medium through which fast-moving market makers can devour less-experienced traders. Creating a stable asset that people will hold, save, and even pass down to their children is a challenge no financial institution has undertaken yet.

This is a good survey of the things you can build with smart contracts and dapps on the Ethereum network, but it's hardly a comprehensive list.

Summary

This is only the beginning of a new world of application development made possible by distributed applications. You'll find more dapp examples and concepts at http://dapps. eth.guide.

Finally, the next chapter covers what's to come for the Ethereum network: future components and the roadmap that guides their development.

■ ■ ■

CHAPTER 11

Advanced Concepts

Where the Ethereum Protocol is going, and where it came from

A book introducing Ethereum and Solidity would not be complete without mention of the nascent cult of personality forming around Vitalik Buterin, the inventor of Ethereum and a collaborator on a handful of other high-profile blockchain projects.

Who Is Leading Software Developers Toward Decentralization?

Perhaps the best description of Buterin comes in the form of an article published about him in Spring of 2014 by writer Morgan Peck in the online magazine Backchannel.[1] The article describes the writer's first encounter with the Ethereum cofounder:

> Buterin was the only person awake. He was sitting outside in a deck chair, working intensely. I didn't bother him, and he didn't say hello. But, I remember the impression he made on me at the time. This skeletal, 19-year-old boy, who was all limbs and joints, was hovering above his laptop like a praying mantis, delivering it nimble, lethal blows at an incredible speed.

> Buterin, it turned out, was the reason everyone was there in the first place. Two months earlier, he had published a white paper describing an impossibly ambitious technology, one that looked beyond Bitcoin's mission of enabling unstoppable, unmediated digital payments, and envisioned a platform for autonomous software of all kinds.

---

[1]Backchannel, "The Uncanny Mind That Build Ethereum," https://backchannel.com/the-uncanny-mind-that-built-ethereum-9b448dc9d14f#.ct4n4b561, 2016.

© Chris Dannen 2017
C. Dannen, *Introducing Ethereum and Solidity*, DOI 10.1007/978-1-4842-2535-6_11

At the center of this free and open source network protocol movement, Buterin's intellectual leadership stands alone. Perhaps the most shocking thing about it, besides the jaw-dropping ambition of the project to replace the HTTP Web with something better, is the speed.

The Ethereum project was launched in 2014, operational by 2015, and was the number two cryptocurrency network after Bitcoin by 2016. The current listing for all Ethereum Foundation members can be found at www.ethereum.org/foundation.

In 2017, the core development team plans to roll out other components that will see Ethereum reach parity with the web applications we know and love today—but with an astounding new set of capabilities like those described in all the previous chapters.

The rest of this chapter concerns the Ethereum roadmap, and some of the yet-unsolved and unbuilt components.

If you'd like to stop here to dig into the mathematics, economics, and business rationale behind the Ethereum network as it works today, you'll find no better place for long, in-depth essays than the Ethereum blog, where Buterin has laid out his thinking about some of the protocol's core concepts.

Vitalik's Best Technical Blog Posts

Following are some interesting blogs to consider:

- https://blog.ethereum.org/2015/06/06/the-problem-of-censorship/

- https://blog.ethereum.org/2015/04/13/visions-part-1-the-value-of-blockchain-technology/

- https://blog.ethereum.org/2015/04/27/visions-part-2-the-problem-of-trust/

- https://blog.ethereum.org/2015/01/10/light-clients-proof-stake/

- https://blog.ethereum.org/2015/01/23/superrationality-daos/

To see a longer list of people and companies contributing to the Ethereum ecosystem, visit http://ecosystem.eth.guide.

The Ethereum Release Schedule

Modern server applications do three things well: they compute and run programs, they remember our data, and they facilitate human interaction. Today, the Ethereum Virtual Machine can compute, but it can't store much data, and it can't serve as an intermediary for messaging between people.

As it happens, the two latter components are in the works as we speak. The near-term Ethereum roadmap consists of three major components:

EVM: Decentralized state (done!)

Swarm: Decentralized storage

Whisper: Decentralized messaging

Whisper (Messaging)

Whisper is a distributed messaging system that is part of the Ethereum protocol and will be available to web applications that use the EVM for their back end. Unlike previous chapters in this book, in which *message* refers to a data object being passed from one smart contract to another, in this case we're using it the old-fashioned way: one human communicating with one or more other humans over a network protocol.

Swarm (Content Addressing)

Swarm is a content-addressed accounting protocol. It works with immutable data, sharding it and storing it across a distributed network in ways that make it easy to recall when an application needs. The goal of Swarm is to be able to find different versions of a file under the same memory address, mimicking domain paths in today's URLs, with their folder structure.

It's important to note that this addressing protocol is hardware-agnostic. It's merely serving the purpose of an index to which chunks of data are stored where. This blob storage scenario is a popular application for decentralized systems, and Swarm would make it even easier, thanks to some of the innovations pioneered by BitTorrent. If you don't want to wait for Swarm, check out an existing distributed file storage protocol called Interplanetary File System, or IPFS, which can also be made to work with Ethereum dapps.

Let's say it's the year 2020 and you visit an Ethereum application in the Mist browser. By this point, let's imagine there's a human-readable namespacing system in place; Ethereum is at full parity with the Web complete with its own domain name lookup system. Here's how the data retrieval process would work with a dapp using the Swarm protocol:

1. Navigate to app in Mist. Enter an Ethereum Domain Name.

2. Domain is translated into a Swarm hash.

3. Swarm retrieves HTML/CSS/JS files linked to this hash.

4. Requests for new files linked to this hash load recent data as it comes in.

For users, the experience won't be much different from using an existing web application. However, the goal here is to achieve P2P storage that is distributed denial of service (DDoS) resistant and offers 100 percent uptime, and can be easily accessed programmatically by all sorts of clients, accessing files on all different storage networks.

You can learn more about Swarm by reading the white paper at `http://swarm-gateways.net/bzz:/swarm/#the-thsph-orange-paper-series`.

What the Future Holds

In Spring 2016, Buterin released a new white paper with the jocular title "Mauve Paper." In this paper he laid out seven primary focal points for the remainder of the Ethereum roadmap:

Transitioning from a proof-of-work to a proof-of-stake consensus algorithm. As a consensus system, proof of work is effective but expensive from a power-consumption perspective. Securing consensus without mining would reduce electricity waste as well as the need for the inflationary issuance scheme.

Faster block times should result from proof of stake, resulting in greater granularity of data and efficiency without a loss of security or risk of centralization.

Economic finality. As covered in Chapter 3, the promise of Ethereum for enterprises is a decentralized system for transaction settlement finality. Proof-of-stake systems might include roles for validator nodes that *fully commit* to a block, meaning they lose their ETH balance (which could be millions of dollars) if they collude to propagate a false block.

Scalability is a problem when full nodes require the computing resources they do today. The large blockchain, 1 GB DAG, and intensive CPU or GPU requirements make smartphones and other low-power devices a no-go for Ethereum node daemons. To read the team's white paper on scalability, visit `https://github.com/vbuterin/scalability_paper/blob/master/scalability.pdf`.

Another vital read about scalability is the use of so-called chain fibers, at `www.reddit.com/r/ethereum/comments/31jm6e/new_ethereum_blog_post_by_dr_gavin_wood/`.

Sharding blockchain data and enabling cross-shard communication is another crucial element of scaling. *Sharding* is the process of breaking up a single chunk of data across databases, in such a way that it can be reassembled when needed. Blockchains don't shard. However, it should be feasible to let different parts of the EVM state be stored by different nodes, and to build applications that can address them there.

Being resistant to censorship in the form of attempts by validator nodes, in a proof-of-work scheme, to collude across all shards in order to block certain transactions from reaching finality. This already exists in Ethereum 1.0, but will be strengthened in subsequent releases.

The Mauve Paper is located at `http://vitalik.ca/files/mauve_paper.html`.

Other Interesting Innovations

As the Ethereum team works toward their vision for the EVM, the Ethereum developer community continues to experiment with solutions of their own. Some promising technical innovations that have attracted attention are as follows:

> *State channels*: Like micropayment channels, a state channel is a link between two blockchain-based databases whereby ledgers are synchronized and updated without needing to wait for the main chain to process the transaction. To read more about how these might work, check out www.jeffcoleman.ca/state-channels/.
>
> *Light clients*: Light clients would allow smartphones and other low-power computers to use the Merkle-Patricia tree—or part of it—to construct a proof showing that a certain transaction is indeed in a block. This would forgo the need to download and synchronize the entire blockchain, but could still validate, send, and receive transactions. To read more about how light clients might work, consult this web archive: https://web. archive.org/web/20140623061815/http://sourceforge. net/p/bitcoin/mailman/message/31709140/.
>
> *Ethereum computation marketplace*: A computation marketplace would be one way to allow some transactions to happen off-chain, and be reconciled to the public chain later. One project experimenting with this approach can be found at https://github.com/pipermerriam/ethereum-computation-market.

Full Ethereum Roadmap

Although software development can be an unpredictable process, the Ethereum developers have been remarkably adept at hitting timeline milestones. Here are the ones they've completed, and those that are yet to come, as of this writing.

Frontier Release (2015)

Frontier had several main goals, all of which were met on time. Everything in this phase of Ethereum was done via the command line. Priorities at the time included the following:

- Getting mining operations running (at a reduced reward rate)
- Getting ether listed on cryptocurrency exchanges
- Establishing a live environment to test dapps

- Creating a sandbox and faucet for acquiring ether

- Allowing people to upload and execute contracts

Homestead Release (2016)

The Homestead release brought many more mainstream cryptocurrency enthusiasts into the fold with the Mist browser. Its characteristics are as follows:

- Ether mining goes up to 100 percent reward rate

- No network halts

- Slightly-less-beta status (fewer warnings)

- More documentation for command line and Mist

Metropolis (2017)

As of this writing, work is underway on Metropolis, the second phase of Ethereum protocol development. This release will be the true coming-out party for Mist, which when fully featured, will look something like a cross between Chrome and the iOS App Store. It will include several heavyweight third-party applications. By this point, Swarm and Whisper will be operational.

Serenity (2018)

This phase is so-named for its planned transition away from proof of work and onto something less hectic: ideally, some form of proof-of-stake algorithm. For now, the tentative code name for Ethereum's POS-based consensus engine is Casper.[2] Although nobody has perfected such a consensus system yet, progress happens by the week, and mathematicians and computer scientists working in this area seem confident a breakthrough is near. Two posts that include background material on this aspect of Ethereum research can be found at the following URLs:

> https://blog.ethereum.org/2015/12/24/understanding-serenity-part-i-abstraction/

> https://blog.ethereum.org/2015/12/28/understanding-serenity-part-2-casper/

Summary

What will the world look like by the time Serenity is released, and proof-of-work mining ends? It's hard to say. But Ethereum, Bitcoin, and other cryptonetworks will have several fairly predictable impacts on business IT.

---

[2]Ethereum Blog, "Introducing Casper, the Friendly Ghost," https://blog.ethereum.org/2015/08/01/introducing-casper-friendly-ghost/, 2015.

One of the great 20th-century economists, Ronald Coase, is famous for his insight that firms exist in the first place to avoid the "transaction costs" of going to the market every day looking for workers. Firms create long-term employment agreements that increase efficiency. But these same bureaucratic processes that increase efficiency among a group of a few dozen workers can become a hindrance at scale, making large firms slow and uncompetitive. As a result, they attempt to find an equilibrium point where the minimal amount of bureaucracy creates maximum efficiency.

For the last 20 years, technology has increased the speed of business, as corporations have developed expertise in large-scale software systems. Of late, great amounts of effort have been put into making these systems more adept at dealing with contractors, consultants, and freelancers. These temporary workers enable companies to spin up teams quickly when demand arises, and spin them back down without needing to lay off full-time employees. The boundaries of the modern company are becoming more permeable. According to a study by the software company Intuit, roughly 40 percent of the American workforce will be "contingent workers" by 2020.[3]

Ethereum promises to bolster the trend. When the entire world can operate within a global transaction singleton that can execute trustless applications, the confines of the office building (or the virtual private network, or the firm itself) become less and less necessary. When compensation packages can easily be composed of a series of if-then statements in a smart contract, the distinction between a salary and a bonus become blurred. The size, age, or location of a company may no longer carry cultural connotations about its trustworthiness or importance. The era of the lifetime employee, the company man or company woman, may be ending.

This shift is being recognized at the highest levels of government and banking. On January 18, 2017, Federal Reserve Chair Janet Yellen was asked about the promise of blockchain technology during a fireside chat held at the Commonwealth Club of California. Her response:

We are looking at its promise in terms of some of the technologies that we use ourselves, and many financial institutions are looking at it. It could make a big difference in the way in which transactions are cleared and settled in the global economy.[4]

A paradigm shift may be in store: first, a period of flux as individuals and businesses come to grips with their freedom to engage in business agreements, some even long-term, with little need for counterparties, and little concern for corporate or even state boundaries. Multimillion-dollar deals may (for a while) still be inked on pen and paper, but how many $1 to $100,000 contracts might be handled by Ethereum machines running boilerplate policies? How many wasted dollars and work hours could be saved? How many disagreements rendered immaterial? How many business agreements might be made more fair and enforceable? Many, no doubt. Ultimately, that is the promise of Ethereum.

---

[3]Intuit, "The Intuit 2020 Report," http://about.intuit.com/futureofsmallbusiness/, 2010.
[4]YouTube, Janet Yellen interview, www.youtube.com/watch?v=ktBgb4xHKGY, 2016.

Index

© Chris Dannen 2017
C. Dannen, *Introducing Ethereum and Solidity*, DOI 10.1007/978-1-4842-2535-6

▨ T, U

▨ V

▨ W, X, Y, Z

Get the eBook for only $4.99!

Why limit yourself?

Now you can take the weightless companion with you wherever you go and access your content on your PC, phone, tablet, or reader.

Since you've purchased this print book, we are happy to offer you the eBook for just $4.99.

Convenient and fully searchable, the PDF version enables you to easily find and copy code—or perform examples by quickly toggling between instructions and applications.

To learn more, go to http://www.apress.com/us/shop/companion or contact support@apress.com.